This is the first book in my 53 years of one sitting... As I read The EDGE, a c stay away from my edges..

Brian Buckley CRM, AAI
Senior Vice President, IOA Insurance
Founder/President, Better Man Ministries
www.ioausa.com
www.bettermanministies.com

...Chris' brutal honesty helps you peel back your layers of vulnerability and rebellion and see yourself as God sees you. Unlike many books I have read, The EDGE is not a guilt trip. It is a grace trip, full of the hope and security that comes from a right relationship with God.

Scott Humphrey
CEO - World Floor Covering of America
www.wfca.org

Wow! I was truly blessed reading The Edge. I actually read it straight through only to put it down for a few minutes to have a talk with God. This is a must read for every man...... The edge is closer than we realize. Thank you Chris for speaking truth...

Marc Mero
Former WWE Wrestling Champion
Founder of Champion of Choices
www.thinkPOZ.org

... I'm very thankful Chris took the time to share his vulnerabilities, and even his devastating choices in The Edge. -- it takes a lot of courage and humility to be transparent about them. I'm thankful for the way he clearly spelled out a plan of action and specific steps for men to live lives of godliness and purity.

Rick Bezet
Lead Pastor of New Life Church of Arkansas and author of Be Real, Because Fake Is Exhausting
www.newlifechurch.tv

To say that The EDGE is a no holds barred look into Christ's journey to the edge, would be an understatement. Chris' transparent confession ... sounds a warning that every man needs to hear, regardless of where they are on their journey. This is a short read that every man needs to invest in for himself.

Ron Cook
Founder and President, Care for Pastors
www.careforpastors.org

Anyone convinced they are unforgivable, will find hope as Chris tells how God has forgiven, healed and restored what the adversary has tried to destroy. Every man needs to read The EDGE... Chris will give you the principles and the courage to keep you from falling.

Alton Garrison
Assistant General Superintendent, Assemblies of God
www.ag.org

Chris Gingrasso is extremely transparent and awfully honest as he invites you to be part of the story of his pain and his lessons learned... a necessary read for every man who honors his name, respects his family, and loves his God.

Pasco A. Manzo
President, Teen Challenge New England & New Jersey
www.tcnewengland.org

No matter how far you've fallen or how many mistakes you've made, God is always there, ready to bring forgiveness and restoration. In The EDGE, Chris takes you on a journey that will challenge you to evaluate your life and encourage you to make a change and embrace the grace of Jesus Christ.

Randy Bezet
Lead Pastor - Bayside Community Church
Bradenton, FL
www.mybayside.church

The EDGE, is one of the most important books I've ever read.. You will be challenged and encouraged. No matter where we fall short, Chris reminds us that it's never too late to follow the greatest guide: Jesus.

I highly recommend this book to any man...

Ronald Joselin
CEO – Inspire International
www.inspireworldwide.com

This book is mesmerizing. Powerfully impacting, intimate and inspirational, I want every man and couple in my church to read The EDGE. This book will help pull many men and women from the edge of destruction and help those who have fallen learn how to be restored and renewed.

Barnie Huie
Lead Pastor Oasis Church
www.ioasis.org

THE EDGE

THE EDGE

Chris Gingrasso

IMPACT PUBLISHING

The Edge

© 2016 by Chris Gingrasso

First Printing, March, 2016

IMPACT PUBLISHING. www.impactfreedom.org

Cover and graphic design by Doni Keene

All Scripture quotations are from the Holy Bible from one of four translations:

The Holy Bible, New International Version®, NIV® Copyright © 1973, 1978, 1984, 2011 by Biblica, Inc.® Used by permission. All rights reserved worldwide.

Scripture quotations marked (NLT) are taken from the Holy Bible, New Living Translation, copyright © 1996, 2004, 2007 by Tyndale House Foundation. Used by permission of Tyndale House Publishers, Inc., Carol Stream, Illinois 60188. All rights reserved.

Scripture taken from the New King James Version. Copyright © 1982 by Thomas Nelson, Inc. Used by permission. All rights reserved.

Scripture quotations taken from the Amplified® Bible, Copyright © 2015 by The Lockman Foundation Used by permission.

ISBN _978-1530206339

Acknowledgments

Thanks to the men of the Dream Builders, an organization that allows me and others to dream together. Kennan Burch, thanks for *always* being my biggest cheerleader. Thanks to Brian Buckley, who actually pushed and pleaded with me to write this book. And to my special friends off of whom I get to bounce my life (good, bad, and at times UGLY): Dan Hobbs, Michael Goss, Jeff Testerman, Jim Tegelhutter, Robbie Wilson, AC Lockyer, and Ronald Joselin. Without you all, I would have just given up LONG ago!

Thank you to Pat Schatzline for not only writing my foreword but standing with me when I felt like I was alone on an island in the middle of nowhere! Thanks, Joe Pici, who called me literally every week, sometimes several times a week, just to check on me. Thanks to Renaut van der Riet for being true to me and allowing me and my family to heal.

And thanks to the folks mentioned, or implied, in this, my story: Rick and Michelle Bezet, Darren Delaune, Bobby Hamilton, and the love of my life and mother of my children, Heather Gingrasso — thanks for saying "Yes" back in 1999!

And I would be amiss if I did not mention my kids, Candace, Kaitlyn, Nathan, and Micah. It is NOT easy being my children, but you all love me for ME ... and I would not trade you kids for all the chocolate on the planet. Thanks also to Frank Gingrasso, my dad, for *always* believing in me.

And most of all, thank you, Jesus! Sometimes I think you must *really* be desperate to use me. I feel your love and am thankful daily for your grace and mercy.

Dedication

I dedicate this book to my amazing wife, Heather! Your ability to forgive and then trust is the most astounding gift anyone could give to another person. I am more in love with you today than EVER before. May these pages that come from the back stage of our lives help others be victorious. And through YOUR example may many women find it in their hearts to also forgive and, better yet, help men to never get too close to, or ever go over, "The Edge"!

I love you!

Chris

CONTENTS

ACKNOWLEDGMENTS	7
DEDICATION	9
FOREWORD	13
INTRODUCTION	17
CHAPTER 1 **THE PATH:** *JESUS STYLE*	21
CHAPTER 2 **THE PLAN:** *WITHOUT HOLES*	27
CHAPTER 3 **THE VIEW:** *A LOOK INSIDE*	31
CHAPTER 4 **THE EDGE:** *MY STORY*	37
CHAPTER 5 **THE BOTTOM:** *GROUND ZERO*	41
CHAPTER 6 **THE TRAVELER:** *BEWARE!*	45
CHAPTER 7 **THE MINISTRY:** *LOCAL CHURCH LIFE*	55

CHAPTER 8
    THE TRIP: *My Guard Down*   59

CHAPTER 9
    THE EDGE: *A Setup*   63

CHAPTER 10
    THE END: *Aharit*   69

CHAPTER 11
    THE BOTTOM: *Part 2*   75

CHAPTER 12
    THE BASIN: *My Heart Revealed*   83

CHAPTER 13
    THE TRUTH: *Who Goes First?*   87

CHAPTER 14
    THE START: *Every Day*   95

CHAPTER 15
    THE ASSIGNMENT: *Old Man...Die!*   99

CHAPTER 16
    THE FACTS: *Mere Men?*   107

CHAPTER 17
    THE HOPE: *Our Guardrails*   113

CHAPTER 18
    THE PROMISE: *Not Cheap Grace!*   117

CHAPTER 19
    THE RESCUE: *HELPING OTHERS UP*   **123**

CHAPTER 20
    THE POSSIBILITY: *TRUE FREEDOM!*   **127**

GREAT BOOKS TO READ   **133**

ABOUT THE AUTHOR   **135**

YOU'RE NOT ALONE...   **137**

Foreword

Pat Schatzline, Evangelist and Author
Remnant Ministries International
www.Remnantintl.com

This book is a must read for every man. My heart was so deeply stirred as I read "The Edge" by my friend and brother, Author Chris Gingrasso. Every single man has at some point gotten too close to "the edge" where destruction is waiting. Chris gets refreshingly and candidly real with the reader about his own fall from grace and to his rise to redemption. This book will force every man to get honest and realize that the "end of yourself is the beginning of God." I am very proud of Chris for being so raw in this message of hope. Now is the time for men to arise and lead with the anointing and courage that only Jesus could give to them. First, I must first bring some warnings to the reader holding this book:

Warning: Do not read this book if you do not want to encounter a reality check with your own heart!

Warning: Do not read this book if you do not want to walk in freedom!

Warning: Do not read this book if you are ok with believing that God cant use the messed up!

Warning: Do not read this book if you do not want to stop hurting your family!

Warning: Do not read this book if you believe that God cannot deliver you!

Why? Because this book will require change! Men we must once again do as Job said in Job 31:1, "I made a covenant with my eyes not to look lustfully at a young woman." We must make up our minds that our conscience will not be seared by the lust of the flesh, but rather we will be knitted together by the love of our Heavenly Father.

This book will take you on a journey from the mirror of self to the cross of freedom. I have traveled the world ministering to tens of thousands and I have seen the destruction of the home first hand. Nearly every story I have encountered could have been avoided if men would choose to arise and take their place as priests in their homes.

I am reminded of the story of Gideon and his sons finally confronting two evil men named Zebah and Zalmunna in **Judges 8**. These evil men had destroyed Gideon's family. Gideon had chased them down and had them cornered. Suddenly, Gideon asked his son to take up the sword and kill Zebah and Zalmunna, but his son Jether was afraid and refused to pick up a sword. (vs. 20). Then the two enemies of Gideon, Zebah and Zalmunna, mocked Gideo by saying in verse 21,"Come, do it yourself. 'As is the man, so is his strength.'"

The story goes onto to say that Gideon arose and slew the two enemies'. This story transcends time and generations.

Men we must be willing to rise and conquer the enemy. We must not expect our children to destroy what we did not. Remember this saying, "As is the man, so is his strength." We must realize that if we do not confront the "Daddy –Demons" then most likely neither will our children.

Finally, Chris teaches us in "The Edge" that "Radical Righteousness" and "Guard Rails" lead to a life of victory! Together we can win the war of the flesh! I say, "Bravo!" to Chris for writing this masterpiece and message of hope! May it be so that men will rise and lead far from "the edge", but in the center of God's will! Now let the healing begin!

Introduction

I have served as a minister for more than 25 years, and in that time I have heard of countless men who have struggled with sin. I have heard stories ranging from men being tempted to gaze upon God's amazing creation jogging in tight shorts in the summer, to men being pulled to stare at porn sites after everyone has gone to bed. I wish it stopped there, but it doesn't. I have heard of men emailing naked strangers and willfully participating in a full-fledged affair. Some struggle with power, others with money. But it seems that all men, everywhere, struggle with something.

I have heard stories like these far too many times. Stories about men. Young men. Old men. Black men and white men. It makes *no* difference! Rich or poor. Thin or obese. A homeless man or a president. A CPA or even a preacher. The sad fact is … ALL men struggle with something.

So let me ask you a personal question — are you ready to get *real?* Are you ready to take off your church mask? Are you ready to look in the mirror and just be honest with yourself? Maybe for the first time … ever.

That is what this book is all about. I am about to take you on a private backstage tour of the mess I mentioned above. The sad fact is, these realities have not only happened to many of the people I have counseled over the years, and they not only have been documented in the

Bible, they also have happened to *ME*.

As I climbed up the ladder, whether it was as a pastor in four churches, as a popular circuit-conference speaker for more than 15 years, as a multi-million-dollar sales rep, or as an executive of a growing global company, I came to realize how many people I can hurt by getting too close to the edge and falling off. I am about to get real candid with you. I am going to give you a backstage pass into my life. To be honest, it's kind of scary! But I know if you will allow God to speak through the pages of this book, my pain can be your gain!

 *The sad fact is ... ALL men struggle with something.*

I have also discovered that there is a progression to sin, as we will discover in the pages that follow. I will use the Scriptures to show the way, the path we should be on. And I will become *very* vulnerable and share my story to help you identify any weaknesses in your life. We see in **Psalm 1**:

> *1 Blessed is the one who does not <u>walk</u> in step with the wicked*
> *or <u>stand</u> in the way that sinners take or <u>sit</u> in the company of mockers,*
> *2 but whose delight is in the law of the Lord, and who meditates on his law day and night.*
> *3 That person is like a tree planted by streams of water, which yields its fruit in season and whose leaf does not wither — whatever they do prospers.*

Introduction

4 Not so the wicked! They are like chaff that the wind blows away.
5 Therefore the wicked will not stand in the judgment, nor sinners in the assembly of the righteous.
6 For the Lord watches over the way of the righteous, but the way of the wicked leads to destruction.

PSALM 1:1-6 NIV (EMPHASIS MINE)

I have discovered that, apparently. God has a path for me to follow. And it is my hope that you soon will understand that He has a path for you as well — a path each of us should take to accomplish His will for our lives. God also gives us clear directions on the path to *not* walk on! He warns us to not <u>*walk*</u> in the steps, not <u>*stand*</u> in the path, nor <u>*sit*</u> in the chair of the mockers. See the progression? It is not immediate. One does not leave the safe zone and then fall off the Edge in a single step. No. It is a process. We are on a path; then we take a step off the course He has chosen for us. If we are not careful, we scurry toward the interesting-looking cliff edge, maybe to get a better "look." But the sad reality is that we end up falling off the edge. Perhaps the worst part of the process is that, when we fall, we hurt everyone we love the most. But there *is* good news: God can and *does* heal. God can and does deliver. And God can and does *set us free*!

> "So Christ has truly set us free. Now make sure that you stay free, and don't get tied up again in slavery to the law."
>
> **GALATIANS 5:1 NLT**

I pray that God, through His Holy Spirit, will take the words in these pages and cause you to literally shudder with the reality that you may be next ... unless you heed these words and _**stay away from the edge**_!

If you saw this sign while on a hike, would you be tempted to go close to the edge and check it out? Probably not. Would you think the sign maker was a fool? Probably not. Why would you trust a random sign from a perfect stranger?

Chapter 1

THE PATH
Jesus Style

For we do not have a high priest who is unable to empathize with our weaknesses, but we have one who has been tempted in every way, just as we are — yet he did not sin.

Hebrews 4:15 NIV

Jesus is the one we are all supposed to imitate, right? Paul says in **Ephesians 5:1 NLT**: *"Imitate God, therefore, in everything you do, because you are his dear children."* (Emphasis mine)

So how in the world did Jesus make it? I know, He was not living on the earth in a time with smartphones, when in privacy, well — literally anywhere — you can look at ... anything. Nor did He have Facebook, where an old girlfriend from high school going through a wicked divorce could send Him her "thoughts." He did not feel the pull to get into a 720-horsepower Lamborghini Aventador, then drive like a crazy man in a "mid-life crisis."

But what Jesus did was not eat a meal for 40 days and 40 nights and become, as the Bible says, "hungry." Let's look at this unreal story in **Matthew 4**:

> *1 Then Jesus was led by the Spirit into the wilderness to be tempted there by the devil.*
> *2 For forty days and forty nights he fasted and became very hungry.*
> *3 During that time the devil came and said to him, "If you are the Son of God, tell these stones to become loaves of bread."*
> *4 But Jesus told him, "No! The Scriptures say, 'People do not live by bread alone, but by every word that comes from the mouth of God.'"*
> *5 Then the devil took him to the holy city, Jerusalem, to the <u>**highest point**</u> of the Temple,*
> *6 and said, "If you are the Son of God, jump off [the Edge]! For the Scriptures say, 'He will order his angels to protect you. And they will hold you up with their hands so you won't even hurt your foot on a stone.'"*
> *7 Jesus responded, "The Scriptures also say, 'You must not test the Lord your God.'"*
> *8 Next the devil took him to the <u>**peak of a very high mountain**</u> [to the edge] and showed him all the kingdoms of the world and their glory.*
> *9 "I will give it all to you," he said, "if you will kneel*

down and worship me."
10 "Get out of here, Satan," Jesus told him. "For the Scriptures say, 'You must worship the Lord your God and serve only him.'"
11 Then the devil went away, and angels came and took care of Jesus.

MATTHEW 4:1-11 NLT (EMPHASIS MINE)

Isn't it interesting that the devil tried three different temptations to destroy Jesus? The first one had to do with Jesus not eating for 40 days, and the devil offered hot rolls dripping with melted butter. I know that is not exactly what it says, but I believe *that* is what Jesus

The devil will always tempt us with what we want and think we need!

heard! The devil will *always* tempt us with what we want and think we *need*! Of course, Jesus won that initial temptation duel by quoting the Word of God out loud to the devil's face.

The remaining two temptations had to do with Jesus coming right to the EDGE. Satan said, "Jesus, come over to the Edge and throw yourself off ..." Jesus never got close to the edge to even see how high they were. He just quoted God's Word. Then Satan said, "Jesus come to the EDGE of this high mountain and look what you can see ..." Once again, Jesus remained far from the EDGE and simply quoted God's Word. Oh yeah, and He told the devil to get out of His face!

The very real enemy desires to take us up so he can have us fall down off the Edge! The way to victory was demonstrated by Jesus more than once. Jesus won — every time! He showed us the way. It is so simple. But ... it is not easy!

I have felt compelled to write this book. Many of my friends have encouraged me to write it. One said after I shared a part of my journey: "Other men *need* to hear this ... they need your realness, your story!" So here I go. I am about to turn the lights on. Why? Because this is what James says:

> *Confess your sins to each other and pray for each other so that you may be healed. The earnest prayer of a righteous person has great power and produces wonderful results.*
> **JAMES 5:16 NLT (EMPHASIS MINE)**

See, now you know. It is my personal prayer for my story, as messy as it is, to not only continue to heal me but, better yet, heal you and thousands of other men just like us. For some of you reading this are right on *your* edge. My sincere hope is that, for others reading who are only beginning their journey, the words on the upcoming pages will change their course forever. Either way, we need to *stay back* from the Edge!

God requires us to *be holy*. In fact, that phrase is used in the Bible some 300 times — 44 times in the book of Leviticus alone, and then 23 times in the book of Acts.

Here is the best part! Jesus is now our high priest who gets it. He gets US!

For we do not have a high priest who is unable to empathize with our weaknesses, but we have one who has been tempted in every way, just as we are — yet he did not sin.

HEBREWS 4:15 NIV

For God called you to do good, even if it means suffering, just as Christ suffered for you. He is your example, and you must follow in his steps.

1 PETER 2:21 NLT

Chapter 2

THE PLAN
Without Holes

For God saved us and called us to live a holy life. He did this, not because we deserved it, but because that was his plan from before the beginning of time — to show us his grace through Christ Jesus.

2 Timothy 1:9 NLT

Yes indeed, God has a perfect plan for each of our lives — a plan that He *knew* we would need: His grace. In fact, *all* of us need His grace! That is why the Father would choose to send His Son to die for our sins.

He has a perfect plan for His chosen people of Israel as well. Listen to His observations from Jeremiah:

> God desires to fill us — the cisterns (temples) — with Himself (Living Water)

> *"For my people have done two evil things: They have abandoned me — the fountain of living water. And they have dug for themselves cracked cisterns that can hold no water at all!*
>
> **JEREMIAH 2:13 NLT**

God mentions that His people have done two evil things. One, they abandoned Him, and in this passage, God refers to Himself as "Living Water." It is interesting that Jesus has a similar conversation with a woman at a well in Samaria when He refers to Himself as the Living Water (see **John 4**).

Second, they dug "cracked cisterns" that could not even hold water. I have read this passage many times, but I think I see it clearer now. God desires to fill us — the cisterns (temples) — with Himself (Living Water). He wants us to drink His Living Water so we never thirst again. The problem is, we have holes. We are cracked, and the "Living Water" cannot remain inside. It keeps spilling out. It is wasted as it gushes out.

Let me put this in even more perspective. I found it interesting that, when you study the word "sincere," it is made up of two Latin words: *sin*, meaning without, and *cere*, meaning wax. Potters in antiquity would mark their wares with this word to distinguish themselves from disreputable vendors who used wax to fill cracks and voids in imperfect vessels. Once the vessels were in use, the wax would melt, rendering the pottery useless. Well-crafted work was therefore "sincere."

> *9 And this I pray, that your love may abound still more and more in knowledge and all discernment, 10 that you may approve the things that are excellent, that you may be **sincere** and without offense till the day of Christ ...*
> **PHILIPPIANS 1:9-10 NKJV (EMPHASIS MINE)**

> *Those who lead blameless lives and do what is right, speaking the truth from **sincere hearts**.*
> **PSALM 15:2 NLT (EMPHASIS MINE)**

> *Let us go right into the presence of God with **sincere hearts** fully trusting him.*
> **HEBREW 10:22A NLT (EMPHASIS MINE)**

I guess you could say holiness needs to be without holes! I recently asked myself: "Am I allowing God to 'leak' out of my insincere heart? Have I covered up my holes with wax, hoping no one will see the real me? Am I just pretending to be what I think others want to see?"

Another interesting fact I discovered was that, back in the day, when people were buying costly pottery, the best way for them to ensure the vessel was sincere was to hold it up to the light. That also is really the only way we can know for sure. Let's not make the mistake of comparing ourselves to another person. God never does that. I need to test my trueness using *His* light to reveal any cracks in me.

God has a plan, and that was in His mind long before He even made mankind … before He ever made me.

> *Even before he made the world, God loved us and chose us in Christ to be holy and without fault in his eyes.*
>
> **EPHESIANS 1:4 NLT**

> *Put on your new nature, created to be like God — truly righteous and holy.*
>
> **EPHESIANS 4:24 NLT**

CHAPTER 3

THE VIEW
A Look Inside

The temptations in your life are no different from what others experience. And God is faithful. He will not allow the temptation to be more than you can stand. When you are tempted, he will show you a way out so that you can endure.

1 Corinthians 10:13 NLT

The year was 2006 and I was living in Arkansas as the vice president of a fast-growing global nutritional company. Things were going great in my life! I was making a six-figure income. I had the car of my dreams. Financially, I was buying things without turning them over to see the price, if you know what I mean. I had a great family and we were involved in leadership with a great new church in the community. I had great Christian friends and a great job traveling the world bringing health and wealth to thousands. Doesn't that sound perfect? Our family portrait looked like one happy, loving, amazing family. We looked great. Everyone was smiling so nicely. One would think it *was* perfect.

The truth was, I was traveling the globe with offices in six counties, and when I was away on these business trips, my mind would often wander. I would struggle and have impure thoughts, especially at night alone in my hotel room. To make things worse, my wife and I were in the process of trying to have another child.

I remember thinking back to my teen years growing up in a small town in Wisconsin. When a couple seemed frustrated about their "struggle" to make a baby, I thought they were crazy! I mean, it seemed like the coolest assignment ever! The fact is, being infertile is anything but cool.

At this time in my life, I had a 15-year-old daughter from my first marriage, as well as a four-year-old daughter from my current marriage to Heather. We wanted another child and did not want as big a gap between our children as was the case with my first two girls. To be honest, it was a burning desire more for my wife than for me.

We would schedule our intimate times, which had become a function — or should I say an obligation — rather than an act fulfilling a passion. It became a task to perform. At least, it felt that way to me. It became a time to "produce." I was to provide half of the ingredients for the baby project. My wife was doing her part ... now it was up to me.

Time after time we would monitor, measure, and then do the "duty." Until this season, I had always enjoyed sex, like most men. But now, after trying to have another baby for almost four years, sex had become less than routine for me. In fact, it became cold and mechanical.

> *Simply telling another another dude that we think someone may be a problem without setting up a game plan to keep from going over the Edge is a fatal mistake.*

Our infertile years became the most stressful time in our married life. I started to grow apart from my wife, and this coldness actually sparked the "need" for me to travel even more. It was not an immediate thing, but one that progressed with the arrival of each piece of disappointing news that there still was no baby. We tried artificial insemination two times, and even the sure-fire method of in vitro fertilization. The reality was that, as I drifted away from my wife, I learned to become like a married single person. We lived together and ate together. But the sad fact was that I had stopped loving Heather many months before.

This all was especially crazy because I still was speaking in local churches. I still was considered a spiritual leader. Well, at least I was playing that "role." I was not full-time on staff at a church, but I was full-time "working" for God, so to speak. I was teaching small groups, preaching occasionally on weekends, and teaching several classes each month in our rapidly growing church.

And I also was traveling the globe with my career, making a great living as a vice president of a multi-million-dollar global company. Then one day, it happened. A few folks from the office and I ate at a local restaurant, and I was captivated by our waitress. She was energetic, extremely cute, and — what I really liked — she laughed at all of my jokes (at least that is what it seemed like to me). I wanted her. No, not for sex! Well, at least not yet. I simply wanted to be with her and to work with her. I wanted to utilize some of her energy for the betterment of the company. But to be honest, I also wanted to have a conversation with her. I mean, she was so nice and … fun. I really believed she would be an awesome addition to our growing team!

A few weeks later, the team and I interviewed her, and she passed every test. She was hired! Coincidentally, the very morning we hired her, I saw an amazing girl with tight black spandex leggings working out in the gym. I remember seeing her, thinking WOW, she is a work of art. Then to my surprise, the girl that I had been in a trance over all morning walked right up to me and said, "I am interviewing with you all today!" No way! I did NOT recognize this waitress in her tight-fitting workout attire.

She began working in the office, and right away I realized this might be a problem. In fact, I even mentioned it to one of my co-workers. I told him to watch me, as I thought she might be a problem for me. He agreed. As far as I was concerned, he was my "accountability."

Note: Simply telling another dude that we think someone may be a problem without setting up a game plan to keep from going over the Edge is a fatal mistake. It is the same as having a very fast car and saying to our guy friend, "Man, this car is really fast. I sure hope I don't get a ticket driving too fast. Or worse, driving it off the edge of a cliff!" If it is just a statement, it is meaningless!

In the past, I had been very open and honest along the way with a great pastor friend, Darren. We both cared so much about each other that we would ask each other some hard questions (see Chapter 13). To be totally honest, at this point in my life, I did not want anyone to get close to the way I was thinking, so I just stayed away. I thought it was a good thing that he was busy building a church, as he did not notice that I was drifting. **<u>BAD!</u>**

I chose to not be close to anyone after a while. When you are in a big church, that is actually easy to do. And when the friends around you are busy, it can be done.

Chapter 4

THE EDGE
My Story

To him who is able to keep you from stumbling and to present you before his glorios presence without fault and with great joy.
— Jude 24 NIV

I knew better! I remember sending the first email to our new hire several weeks after we started working together. I simply gave her my cell number with the note: "Here is my cell ... you know ... if there is ever anything you need..." I was creeping to the edge of a cliff, but I had no idea what was over the edge.

You may be wondering why I would do that. Well, it was quite simple. She paid attention to me. She laughed at all my jokes. She noticed me. It felt good to be around her. You see, as I mentioned earlier, I had distended my heart from my wife, and our relationship was very strained. I did not know how bad it really was until it was too late. Without going into all the details, I made up my mind, and the new girl and I scheduled a time to "get together." That was the start of a path leading me right off the Edge! I am sad to say that what began as seemingly innocent emails became a full-blown affair.

Here is the BIG problem. Aside from the fact that I am and was a married man, I still was a regular speaker in our church! The confusing part was that God seemed to still use me when I spoke. His Word went forth, and people were touched. I believe that I was very much like Samson after he had been with Delilah:

> 20 Then she cried out, "Samson! The Philistines have come to capture you!" When he woke up, he thought, "I will do as before and shake myself free." **But he didn't realize the Lord had left him**.
> 21 So the Philistines captured him and gouged out his eyes. They took him to Gaza, where he was bound with bronze chains and forced to grind grain in the prison.
>
> **JUDGES 16:20–21 (EMPHASIS MINE)**

This may be one of the saddest lines in the whole Bible! Samson did not even realize the Lord had left him. The fact is, I did not either. I simply was going through the motions so others would not ask any questions. Even if they had, I was sure not going to ruin what I had worked so hard to set up. I had a plan. It was perfect. Or so I thought. I even packed my bags and moved out.

> *It is astounding how my actions could hurt so many people!*

I took my teenage daughter with me, and we got a small two-bedroom apartment. Things were *bad*!

My wife had no idea about my new relationship at first. Then, one night, God spoke to her in a dream. Like — how does *that* happen? She woke up and knew the girl's name and what I had done. She did not talk to anyone, but God revealed it to her in a dream. I sure did not see *that* coming!

The next morning, she confronted me on the phone, and I confessed that her allegations were true. She was devastated. This started a spiral of hurt that would spread like a tsunami to impact everyone I cared about.

One of the hardest moments of my life came when I decided to confess what I had done to the lead pastor and the executive pastor of the church where I was ministering. These men were my good friends! They trusted me. Man, that hurt worse than I expected. Seeing their faces, so disappointed, so hurt. I spoke to each of them individually and shared what I had done. One pastor wanted to punch me in the face. I am glad he didn't! That day, I resigned from the small group that Heather and I had been leading. My co-leader was brought up to speed about the developments, and he was devastated! It is astounding how my actions could hurt so many people!

Chapter 5

THE BOTTOM
Ground Zero

Whatever you have said in the dark will be heard in the light, and what you have whispered behind closed doors will be shouted from the housetops for all to hear!
— Luke **12:3** NLT

When you are numb, it is hard to feel any pain. About two days after the reality of what had happened finally sunk fully into my wife's mind, I received an email at work that caught my attention. It read something like "How could you do this to me? I cannot take it anymore…please take care of Kaitlyn …"

I remember seeing those words. At that moment, everything switched into slow motion. I wonder what she means by this? I pondered. Then I felt prompted to call my pastor. I read him the note, and he screamed out loud to me, "Call 911 NOW!"

That got my attention even more. Oh no, I hope nothing worse happens... I called 911, and they questioned me profusely and said they would send someone over right away. I immediately left my office, which was about 18 minutes away, and headed to our home to see what in the world was going on.

Unbeknownst to me, my wife had written a letter to our five-year-old daughter, which I later found on our computer. The note instructed her to listen to Daddy, and said that Mommy loved her very much. She said she would miss her but would see her again someday. Then, my hurting wife took the gun her dad had given her for protection years before, and attempted to load it with bullets. She had decided to end her life, her decision fueled by all the hurt and pain I had caused.

I will never forget the sight when I arrived at my house. It was surrounded by four police cars with lights flashing. I dashed inside to find a group of people in my home. It was chaos. People were crying, and then I noticed my wife's body, all curled up on the couch in a fetal position — not crying, simply convulsing with tears. The hardest crying I have ever heard. She was hyperventilating. The hurt on her face ran all though her whole body, like she had been shocked with a grief gun.

The only good news came when I was told that the gun she tried to use did not get loaded properly and did not fire. I have never been more thankful for anything in my life! I cannot imagine how it all would have played out had she been able to load the gun and fulfill her desire.

> *We began to fall in love with each other again, and we started to climb back up the side of the cliff. Slowly.*

The New Day

The next day, our pastor and his wife cleared their schedules and we spent six hours digging though the *why*. The *what* was not as important. I think too many people focus on the details of the what and miss the reasons for what happens. If you do not deal with the *why*, the *what* may very well happen again!

I was so humbled. My pastor and his wife tirelessly worked with me and my hurting wife for days, digging through my now calloused heart and into the reasons we were struggling. It hurt to share some things, and other times it felt like a 1,000-pound weight was being lifted from my chest. I will never forget the first time Heather and I were alone after the first "come back to Jesus" session. We talked for hours — it was amazing! We began to fall in love with each other again, and we started to climb back up the side of the cliff. Slowly. Steadily. Together!

Piece by piece, God began to put our marriage back together. Our love for each other grew stronger every day, and our devotion to God grew as well. I am so thankful for His grace and His mercy, not to mention Heather's amazing forgiveness! Now, years later, we share our story of hope with couples. If we can make it, so can *you*!

My wife is the most amazing woman of God I know. She forgave me, and God is back on the throne in our lives and our marriage. I did not realize how good life could — *should* — be!

CHAPTER 6

THE TRAVELER
BEWARE!

God's will is for you to be holy, so stay away from all sexual sin.
1 Thessalonians 4:3 NLT

After all the pain I caused and the realization that I had strayed from God, I began devouring books. I wanted to know everything there was to know about living a holy life for God. There are many great books out there (I have several listed in the "Great Books to Read" section) written with the purpose of keeping men from sinning. They desire for men to live "holy" lives.

The Bible, of course, also is filled with stories of real men and their struggles. Some of the stories relate accounts of men overcoming their temptations, but most did not. Perhaps the one I identify with the best is the story of King David.

If you are unfamiliar with the story, the basics are that David was on his palace roof when he should have been with his men fighting on the battlefield. One night, when David was alone on the roof, he walked to the Edge and saw a beautiful woman. He desired her. The bathing beauty's name was Bathsheba. She was a married woman and, in fact, David knew her husband. What was he to do?

Well, he had some of his men get her and bring her to his palace and into his chamber. There, he took advantage of her, and as it turned out, she got pregnant! Yep … it only takes *one* time.

After David discovered that Bathsheba was with child, he tried to cover his tracks. David put a plan together to have Bathsheba's husband sleep with her so that, when the baby arrived, it would make sense, and he would think it was his. The only trouble was that Uriah, Bathsheba's husband, was in the king's army and was not at home. So David sent for Uriah to give a "report" about how the battle was going, and he was brought to the palace. After the report of how things were going, David got Uriah drunk and said, "Go spend some time with your wife." Uriah was such a great man that he actually slept on the sidewalk! If the other men could not hook up with their wives, Uriah did not feel it would be fair for him to either.

David tried to get Uriah to sleep with his wife a second time! When that plan failed two times, David finally sent word to have Uriah sent to the front of the battle, where he would surely be killed. **2 Samuel 11:14–15 NIV** tells us, *"In the morning David wrote a letter to Joab and sent it with Uriah. 15 In it he wrote, 'Put Uriah out in front where the fighting is fiercest. Then withdraw from him so he will be struck down and die.'"*

We are then brought into a chain of events that ends with a confrontation between the prophet Nathan and the king of Israel. Let's go over this story, as I want to point out a powerful truth that can help each of us avoid the Edge!

> 1 The Lord sent Nathan to David. When he came to him, he said, "There were two men in a certain town, one rich and the other poor.
> 2 The rich man had a very large number of sheep and cattle,
> 3 but the poor man had nothing except one little ewe lamb he had bought. He raised it, and it grew up with him and his children. It shared his food, drank from his cup and even slept in his arms. It was like a daughter to him.
> 4 "Now a **traveler** came to the rich man, but the rich man refrained from taking one of his own sheep or cattle to prepare a meal for **the traveler** who had come to him. Instead, he took the ewe lamb that belonged to the poor man and prepared it for the one who had come to him."
> 5 David burned with anger against the man and said to Nathan, "As surely as the Lord lives, the man who did this must die!
> 6 He must pay for that lamb four times over, because he did such a thing and had no pity."
> 7a Then Nathan said to David, "You are the man!
> **2 Samuel 12:1–7 NIV (emphasis mine)**

I find it interesting that Nathan used a story to get David's attention. Why not just say, "You bum, I know what you did ... and so does God"?

As I understand it, David was about 48-52 years old when this happened with Bathsheba. I really connect with David here. I also know what it is like to think it, go for it, and then realize — *Oh my! Now what am I going to do?* So David put together this elaborate plan, and he no doubt thought he had covered his tracks. I mean, who was going to know, especially back then? There were no cameras, no email trails, no texting files to examine. So how could anyone ever know?

Apparently David did not notice this in Scripture (Okay, it was not written yet for him to see.):

> *2 The time is coming when **everything that is covered up will be revealed, and all that is secret will be made known to all.***
> *3 Whatever you have said in the dark will be heard in the light, and what you have whispered behind closed doors will be **shouted from the housetops for all to hear!***
>
> **LUKE 12:2–3 NLT (EMPHASIS MINE)**

David forgot about the all-seeing, all-knowing Lord God Jehovah!

The one participant in the story who stands out to me is this "traveler." After analyzing the story, I realized each character represented a specific person. The rich man was David. The poor man was no doubt Uriah. I suspect that the ewe lamb was Bathsheba, but then there

THE TRAVELER BEWARE!

is this other character. If this traveler had not been permitted to enter the house, the man in the story would never have been tempted to provide him with the poor man's lamb.

So who is this "traveler"? I have four possible suggestions for who this "traveler" might be. Number one, the devil. Now, I know the devil is involved with many peoples' challenges. But he is not omnipresent. He can only be in one place at a time. I do not believe this traveler is the devil.

Number two, demons. Yes, they are very real, and many men have fallen under the allure of demonic traps. More on this later. But as real and as powerful as the demonic forces are, I do not believe the traveler represents demons.

Number three, your family past. Again, this is very real. We know that **Exodus 20:5, Exodus 34:7**, and **Numbers 14:18** say that God lays the sins of the parents upon their children; the entire family is affected — even the third and fourth generations of children from those who reject Him. That should cause all of us fathers to cringe right where we are! But as real as this is, I do not believe the traveler in this story to be the DNA of a family.

And finally, number four, friends. That has *got* to be it! So many of us have been led down a path to ruin by the wrong friends. They push us. They prod us. No matter what our age, our friends' influence on our lives is very real. But I do not really believe the character of the "traveler" Nathan was referring to was any of these.

If we could just identify who he is, that would solve the problem. Are you ready? I believe that the traveler is ONE THOUGHT! "What?" you say. "How is that possible?" Well, every action begins with one thought, whether good or bad.

We talk to ourselves with just one thought: "What if..." or "Can you imagine..." or "I wonder..."

Before "the traveler" would leave David's house, he would be an adulterer, a murderer, a liar, and a deceiver. This "man after God's own heart" had opened up his door and let in a stranger, a traveler! I say, <u>*beware of the traveler*</u>!

Just for the record: You will always be tempted. You never get to the place where you will no longer be tempted, at least not while you are alive! James, the brother of Jesus, has this to say about temptation:

> *13 And remember, when you are being tempted, do not say, "God is tempting me." God is never tempted to do wrong, and he never tempts anyone else.*
> *14 Temptation comes from our <u>**own desires**</u>, which entice us and drag us away.*
> *15 These desires give birth to sinful actions. And when sin is allowed to grow, it gives birth to death.*
> **JAMES 1:13–15 NLT (EMPHASIS MINE)**

Yikes, this one hurts. It makes *us* take the responsibility for our actions and not have the right to blame another person! And do you see the progression? Temptation→Entice→Drag away→Give birth to sin→Sin GROWS→Brings DEATH! Death is always the final payment for sin. **Romans 6:23** says, *"For the wages of sin is death, but the free gift of God is eternal life through Christ Jesus our Lord."*

Perhaps one of the biggest challenges in the times in which we live in the fact that judgment is not immediate. I mean, if the wages of sin is death, then when we sin, we should die ... and we will. But God always allows time for His grace to be utilized. This goes way back to the garden, when Adam and Eve sinned against God. God came looking to talk with Adam and Eve after they ate of the fruit of the tree of knowledge of good and evil.

God even asked them if they had eaten from the Tree of Knowledge (**Genesis 3:11**). He gave them a chance to fess up, but they did not. Then an idea entered Eve's mind; she desired to be like God and make herself wise. She had one thought. That is where it started — even *before* Satan started to talk with her.

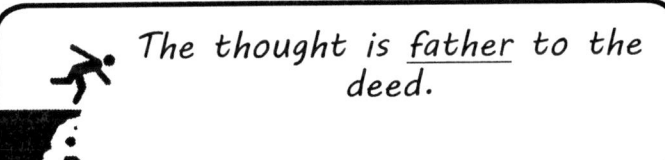

The thought is _father_ to the deed.

BEWARE OF THE TRAVELER!

I have learned that my mind is the starting blocks for all of my actions. When I allow a thought to take root in my mind, I give it permission to grow into an action. You see, that is exactly what happened when I stepped over the Edge and had the affair. My actions first grew from many private thoughts that I played with over and over again in my mind — until I actually got the courage to step closer to the edge.

> *But I am afraid that just as Eve was deceived by the serpent's cunning, your minds may somehow be led astray from your sincere and pure devotion to Christ.*
>
> **2 Corinthians 11:3 NIV**

> *So prepare your minds for action and exercise self-control.*
>
> **1 Peter 1:13a NLT**

The thought is *father* to the deed.

> *12 And so, dear brothers and sisters, I plead with you to give your bodies to God because of all he has done for you. Let them be a living and holy sacrifice — the kind he will find acceptable. This is truly the way to worship him. 2 Don't copy the behavior and customs of this world, but let God transform you into a new person by changing the way you think. Then you will learn to know God's will for you, which is good and pleasing and perfect.*
>
> **Romans 12:1–2 NLT**

Some translations use the word "renew." I like this word too, as it suggests something like renewing your book at the library. Start again afresh. But, really, it is a change-out. Our minds are complex things. If I am honest, I would say now that all sin starts in the mind. MINE!

Apostle Paul says in his second letter to the Corinthian church:

> We demolish arguments and every pretension that sets itself up against the knowledge of God, and we **take captive every thought** to make it obedient to Christ.
> **2 Corinthians 10:5 NIV (emphasis mine)**

Well, this means that I have responsibility! When I do *my* part, then God does His part. Check this out:

> 22 throw off your old sinful nature and your former way of life, which is corrupted by lust and deception.
> 23 Instead, let the Spirit renew your thoughts and attitudes.
> 24 Put on your new nature, created to be like God — truly righteous and holy.
> **Ephesians 4:22–24 NLT**

The battleground is the mind. The outcome of the battle depends on whether I yield to the flesh or the spirit. Paul says:

> 5 Those who are dominated by the sinful nature think about sinful things, but those who are controlled by the Holy Spirit think about things that please the Spirit.
> 6 So letting your sinful nature control your mind leads to death. But letting the Spirit control your mind leads to life and peace.
> 7 For the sinful nature is always hostile to God. It never did obey God's laws, and it never will.
> **Romans 8:5–7 NLT**

What am I feeding? The spirit or the flesh? This is the simple truth: Whatever I feed will be the biggest, and whatever I exercise will be the strongest. So the question is, what am I feeding and exercising — my flesh or my spirit?

Beware of the traveler!

I am making a strong decision: I will not even let him past the front door! I remember times when he was knocking. I was curious. I, of course, did not want to be rude. I peeked through the peep hole. He seemed nice enough. What harm could it be? I love meeting new people. Just open the door a little. It has been locked for years, but now I find a way to justify unlocking the door. Then the knob turns ... it will be okay. What could happen?

BONUS: Did you ever wonder who Uriah was? Let me ask this question: Who do you think could have a house close enough to the king's palace? A total stranger? NO. I suspect that Uriah and Bathsheba had been to the palace to play cards a time or two. You see, David had a group of loyal soldiers that we know as David's Mighty Men. Uriah was one of those 30! Notice that Uriah did not find it strange to be invited to the king's palace. He did not even seem to find it strange to stay for dinner and some wine. I believe it had happened before.

So why is this significant? Well, I believe David had planned this activity for a while. After all, David knew that Bathsheba's husband was out on a mission. *His* mission! In my opinion, it was all done in the *first degree*!

Chapter 7

THE MINISTRY
Local Church Life

You have heard me teach things that have been confirmed by many reliable witnesses. Now teach these truths to other trustworthy people who will be able to pass them on to others.

2 Timothy 2:2 NLT

I stayed at the corporate position for about a year after the affair. I should have been fired, but was not let go. After I resigned, I was uncertain where to go and what to do. My wife and I had saved up some money to live on comfortably, and I was not in a hurry to simply plug back into some corporate gig. About 18 months into my time away from corporate America, Heather and I felt drawn to come to central Florida to return to full-time ministry. Okay, more me than her. But she came with me, thank God. She says she was just being submissive. We both feel that God tricked us.

> *The most important part of any building is the foundation.*

We ended up moving from Arkansas, the only state Heather had ever known, to central Florida as I accepted the position of lead pastor of a very small church. At first, it seemed fun and exciting, but that lasted about a week or so. What a challenge this would become! The most important part of any building is the foundation. Well, this church's foundation was not only cracked, but seemingly built on sand. After being there a short time, we noticed the church was made up of stragglers from other area churches, since the founding pastor also was a former lead pastor from the city. He had left for a few years and then came back to start this new work.

What made matters worse was the horrible financial condition of this church. We ended up using tens of thousands of dollars of our own money just to keep it going in that first year. But, of course, we all know God is faithful. We had been pastoring there for nearly two years when, one day, we felt the release to move on. I left the now-stabilized body of about 100 or so people to a new pastor, a great friend from Bible college who had come down from Minnesota to help us with this ministry. To this day, he has done an amazing job loving the surrounding community, as well as giving God first place in every service and outreach.

For about five weeks, my wife and I prayed and asked God what He wanted us to do next. That's when I received a text from an area pastor that said, "Do we need to talk?" We did, and I took a staff position with a growing multi-campus church. I was quite familiar with the workings of a multi-campus church, as we had left a great one in Arkansas years before. Actually, it was named "the fastest growing church in America" that year by *Outreach Magazine*.

Without being too particular, my time in this position wore me out. I had no idea how much healing I needed until months after I left. It was a combination of being in the wrong position and me not fulfilling my role as a leader. As challenging as it was, however, it was also wonderful in many ways. One of the best features were some of the great people I was blessed to work with. I got to do many fun and exciting things, like produce two TV shows, direct countless video projects, and lead a creative team of really amazing people.

The problem was that I was working more on tasks than with people, and I love people. So it was with mixed emotions that I made the announcement that I was leaving the church. Since I had come on staff, the church had grown to over 5,500 in weekly attendance. We had added two more campuses and were in the process of adding yet another at the time of my leaving.

But I knew I was finished there. Now, once again, I did not have a job to move into, nor did I have another opportunity set in stone. It seems like the story of my life! My poor wife! What I call "faith," she calls frivolous!

Here is the cool thing though. The day I resigned from my position with the church, I received a call from a friend who was interested in me working with his company. I had performed his wedding the previous year and he needed someone like me to help with sales and marketing for two of his companies. I really liked this guy! I loved his work ethic and his creativity. I knew I could help him, and I felt he could help me. Without praying or asking Heather what she thought, I accepted a position.

I loved the idea of going back into the business world. The local church had worn me out. And perhaps the worst part was that I was feeling like a professional Christian. Now, if you are full- or part-time in the local church ministry, please do not be offended by that term. But to be honest, I think lots of ministers have become what I will call a "Professional Christian." That's when we do ministry because it is our job, rather than an outflow from our lives.

We know we are going to struggle when we do things for God. That puts all the pressure on us. I have since learned to do things from God instead. Then He is the initiator, and He is responsible for the outcome.

I took a few weeks off at Christmas, and then I began my new position in the sales world on January 1. With my new adventure, I was about to make a huge life change. I just had no idea how huge it would be.

Chapter 8

THE TRIP
My Guard Down

There is a path before each person that seems right, but it ends in death.
PROVERBS 16:25 NLT

My first travel trip back in the "real world" was to Washington, D.C. It came at the end of my second day back in the sales world. One minute I was "Pastor Chris" on TV — maybe I was being asked to lead a marketing team or even speak to thousands. The next minute I was alone in an unfamiliar hotel room away from what I had grown comfortable with for the last several years.

Traveling was something I had gotten used to for years! In fact, over the years, I have traveled hundreds of thousands of miles, and to avoid trouble, I had a solid routine that I have followed every time I was away from my family in a hotel room. Here it is:

- Never travel alone.
- Have a picture of my family on the night stand and desk.
- Never turn on the TV at night (have adult stations blocked at check in).
- Pray over the room upon entering. (You never know what took place there last night!)
- Call and text family during the day, and tuck my wife in and pray for the family nightly.
- Go to bed early and get up early to pray and listen to worship music.
- Pray for open doors and to be focused and safe.
- Share any temptations with my Mastermind friends (preferably at the time of).

Especially since my affair — nearly ten years ago as I write this book — this routine needed to be followed for sure! That was my plan. The first trip played out just like the old days. I was like a pilot doing a pre-flight check. I even Facetimed with the kids and Heather every morning. That was a nice addition to my travel routine since the last time I traveled.

You see, traveling had been a way of life for me for over 15 years. I had traveled hundreds of thousands of miles, been to several countries, and stayed at countless hotels — all without a hitch. Now that I am going to start traveling again, I thought to myself, I should re-engage in the disciplines I *designed* to protect myself all those years!

> I had a solid routine that I have followed every time I was away from my family in a hotel room.

Then I took another trip. Same thing. I followed my plan and had a great trip with no flesh issues. Easy, I thought. I can do this! Maybe it is not like it was in the past. Maybe I will no longer struggle with my mental wanderings at night alone in my room. Maybe I will not struggle with any lust. I actually started to get very comfortable about traveling.

Until one strange night when I received an email on my personal email account. The email said that they were responding to my Craig's List ad.

"Craig's List ad, I thought? I don't have a Craig's List ad. It was from a woman, and at first I thought nothing of it. I must admit, I felt a faint check from the Holy Spirit. Like CAUTION ... It had been a very long time since I had let my eyes look at anything unclean. Years in fact! I mean, I was a pastor just several months ago!

I usually just delete emails like that. It was spam, of course. But this one seemed "different." Or so I thought. I read it like four times and then it got me. I scrolled down to discover at the bottom of this email a few revealing pictures of this stranger. She, of course, was beautiful. I immediately felt horrible. I mean, I am away from my amazing sweetheart, on a trip, but I was alone. In this lonely room. What harm could one look do? How about two? Wow ... I forgot how amazing these pictures could be. The nice lady in the email said that those pictures were nothing and I should check out some "special" ones at this attached link.

Now keep in mind, I was using my new company's computer. I am not stupid. I am *not* going to go to a porn site. Oh wait, this was Craig's List. That is OK I guess. That is when it happened. You see, there is a "Personal" section on there that gives you options, like a walk down the red light district in Amsterdam! I had NO idea how entrapping that bad decision would turn out to be!

CHAPTER 9

THE EDGE
A Setup

For God's will was for us to be made holy by the sacrifice of the body of Jesus Christ, once for all time.
HEBREWS 10:10 NLT

Anything I want at my fingertips. WOW! I simply could not believe it. My curiosity started to move me closer and closer to the Edge! I reasoned to myself, it would be OK because, I mean, I am NOT going to do anything. I just want a peek over the edge, that's all. I began to creep toward the Edge. Now, I had NO idea it was an edge.

I rationalized that I was no longer "Pastor Chris." I was no longer speaking regularly in a church and was no longer doing Christian TV shows. I convinced myself I was just a guy on a business trip. For the record, at this very moment in this story, believe it or not, I was totally in love with my wife! We had a solid marriage, not to mention I really was in love with Jesus as well. I just stopped doing the little things that I knew to do to keep me away from the Edge.

Growing up as a teen, I was involved in performances of magic professionally in night clubs and the like, so much of what I was around involved alcohol. But believe it or not, I never drank alcohol much at all. And for sure, I have never been drunk; I thought that was taboo. To be honest, I was always afraid what would happen if I let alcohol take too much control of my thoughts. Well, I was about to discover that as well.

But I knew better. For some reason, the pull seemed to be more powerful than I could handle, even though I know the Scripture says:

> *No temptation has overtaken you except what is common to mankind. And God is faithful; he will not let you be tempted beyond what you can bear. But when you are tempted, he will also provide a way out so that you can endure it.*
> **1 Corinthians 10:13 NIV**

 *Now, I had NO idea it was an edge.*

The Perfect Storm

One week I was in Las Vegas doing a trade show for my new company. There were three of us from the company, but for some reason, we were all at separate hotels. The trade show was going great though. We had all kinds of amazing hot business leads coming in, maybe better than ever before.

Then, on a Wednesday, after the showroom closed for the day, a little after 6 p.m., I was scheduled to meet some old friends that used to work with me in Arkansas. They met me at my hotel, and we drove downtown to the old part of Las Vegas. We walked all over Fremont Street. I'm not sure if you have ever done that at night, but as a suggestion, do *not* take your kids! There are crazy people all over that place! I saw Elvis. Yep, he is living in Vegas now. Superman was shorter than I envisioned. And best of all, an 80-plus-year-old man in a diaper. That is all he was wearing! Wow, I could have gone my whole life and not seen that in person!

After waiting for an hour to get seated, we ate at an amazing Thai restaurant and had great conversation while catching up. Everything seemed wonderful until I tried some of the appetizer. It was so good at first; then I got some kind of pepper from hell. No, really. My mouth was on *fire*! I took a sip of the Coke I had ordered, but it did nothing. The person I was next to was drinking some minty-type drink. I asked if I could try it. It soothed my tongue, so I took two big gulps. We finished our meal and walked around some more, and then they took me back to my hotel. As I said, I am not a drinker. I had started to drink wine, but only when I traveled because my wife hates anything to do with alcohol.

I was not used to all the standing at those trade shows! So after dinner, I was more than ready to call it a night. When I got back to my room I noticed I had received an invitation from the Craig's List woman. She wanted to meet up with me? Really? THAT is crazy! But I must say, at that very moment, it felt kind of cool. We had a very short dialogue. That is when one of the strangest things happened to me. I got cold all over. Like a winter breeze had come into the room. I actually had to turn the heat on! I have felt this before, and it always had to do with the demonic.

She then asked how "generous" I was. What? What does THAT mean? Oh wait. Yikes, I have been conversing with a person who charges for sex! You have GOT to be kidding me! Maybe I knew it. Maybe I felt the rush of it all. Her fee? $200 for an hour. Now *that* is crazy! Luckily, I do not carry much cash with me when I travel as I put it all on a credit card because it is easier to keep up with the expenses. I mean, I will NEVER meet up with a prostitute. That is sick! Not to mention, they charge money. But worse, they may have diseases! And there is NO way I would hurt my wife again! Especially since we are doing so good.

THE EDGE A SETUP

I must confess, it was exhilarating. I know, I got right to the edge...looked over...and realized I was in trouble. Good thing she got frustrated with me as I was not going to give her my room number, nor come see her at her place! I was not making her any money. She said I was wasting her time. That was it. The communication stopped.

I decided to take a shower. When I got out, I was feeling mighty sick from the food, but because of the new journey to the edge I was feeling quite spunky, if you know what I mean. This is when I lost my mind. For the first time in our 15 years of marriage, I decided to send a sexy text to my wife, who was back in Florida. Somehow, in my current state of mind and mixed with the alcohol that I was not used to, sending a picture of myself naked seemed like the thing to do.

Yep, I sent the text. I believe I had a silly smirk on my face when I hit send, all the while wondering what she would think of ...*that*. Then I was off to bed. About 10 to 15 minutes later, I felt awful and needed to use the restroom. I realized that I had not plugged my phone in for the night, so I stopped by to plug it in, and when I did, it lit up. That is when I realized that I did not send a text of myself (in a rather provocative pose) to my wife. Instead, it went to the general manager of my company, who, incidentally, was a woman!

I was stunned! How could I have done this? Oh no! Of *all* people! I wanted to die right there. It was like ice cold water being poured all over me. No ... it was like *acid* was being poured over me! That is when I sensed a laugh from the enemy, and I literally heard the words

"You are finished now!" Those words pierced my heart. What had I just done? I had just fallen off the Edge ... _**again**_!

CHAPTER 10

THE END
AHARÌT

For lack of discipline they will die, led astray by their own great folly.
PROVERBS 5:23 NIV

A number of years ago, I had the privilege of hearing Dr. Michael Brown speak at a men's conference in Pensacola, Florida. Brownsville Assembly was in the middle of an amazing revival that lasted for many years. Dr. Brown spoke on a subject that captured my attention. Being a Hebrew scholar, he introduced the group of men to a powerful word: 'Aharìt (pronounced ah-kha-REET).

In fact, his book, *Go and Sin No More,* is a masterpiece on how to stop sinning, as he deals with the reality of the 'Aharìt'. He says, "The word for 'Aharìt is related to the Hebrew word for 'back,' and it literally means 'that which comes after; after-effects; final consequences; end'" (p. 77).

The word 'Aharìt occurs sixty-five times in the Old Testament, and thirteen of those can be found in the book of Proverbs, such as in **Proverbs 19:20 NIV**: I discovered *"Listen to advice and accept discipline, and at the <u>end</u> you will be counted among the wise"* (emphasis mine).

Perhaps the best usage of this is found in **Proverbs 5:**

> *1 My son, pay attention to my wisdom; listen carefully to my wise counsel.*
> *2 Then you will show discernment, and your lips will express what you've learned.*
> *3 For the lips of an immoral woman are as sweet as honey, and her mouth is smoother than oil.*
> *4 But <u>in the end</u> she is as bitter as poison, as dangerous as a double-edged sword. 5 Her feet go down to death; her steps lead straight to the grave.*
> *6 For she cares nothing about the path to life. She staggers down a crooked trail and doesn't realize it.*
> **PROVERBS 5:1–6 (EMPHASIS MINE)**

Once I know what to look for, it becomes so easy to see. Like when Heather and I were thinking about getting a minivan. I, of course, did not want one of those! I wanted an SUV or something. So we started to discuss the possibilities of a minivan, and it seemed like people all over the place were getting vans and then driving them in front of us. The reality was we were focused on minivans, and we simply become more aware of them. That is how it must be with the *'Aharìt*.

Here is what **Proverbs 7** shares about the end:

> 21 So she seduced him with her pretty speech and enticed him with her flattery.
> 22 He followed her at once, like an ox going to the slaughter. He was like a stag caught in a trap,
> 23 awaiting the arrow that would pierce its heart. He was like a bird flying into a snare, little knowing it would cost him his life.
> **PROVERBS 7:21–23 NLT**

If only I had seen the 'Aharìt! If only I had paid caution to the Holy Spirit's warning.

Get the picture? Reading this took me back to the time I was at a slaughterhouse. When I was 14 or so, my friend and I rode our bikes about 20 miles into the Wisconsin countryside to visit a real slaughterhouse. It was surreal! I have never witnessed anything like that. It almost makes me want to become a vegetarian…until I smell bacon or steak on the grill!

These cows had no idea what awaited them around the corner. They were all lined up — then BANG. One by one, they were taken down. Their blood was drained, and they were cut up for meals. THAT is the visual God gives us about heading over the Edge.

I now realize this not only pertains to sexual things, but to alcohol as well. Like it says in **Proverbs 23:**

> *29 Who has anguish? Who has sorrow? Who is always fighting? Who is always complaining? Who has unnecessary bruises? Who has bloodshot eyes?*
> *30 It is the one who spends long hours in the taverns,*
> *31 Don't gaze at the wine, seeing how red it is, how it sparkles in the cup, how smoothly it goes down.*
> *32 For* **in the end** *[literally 'Aharìt] it bites like a poisonous snake; it stings like a viper.*
> *33 You will see hallucinations, and you will say crazy things.*
> *34 You will stagger like a sailor tossed at sea, clinging to a swaying mast.*
> *35 And you will say, "They hit me, but I didn't feel it. I didn't even know it when they beat me up. When will I wake up so I can look for another drink?"*
>
> Proverbs 23:29–35 NLT

If only I had seen the *'Aharìt*! If only I had paid caution to the Holy Spirit's warning.

My End

After I realized I had sent a *very* inappropriate text to my GM, I immediately texted her back saying I was so sorry and that was not intended for her. But the damage was done.

That was Wednesday night. I flew home on Saturday. I must say, walking into the office Monday morning

THE END Aharit

was awkward. We had just had one of the most fulfilling and, possibly, most financially rewarding trade shows in the history of the company. Many millions of dollars of new business would soon be contracted and written.

Right after lunch, I was called out of my office and into the owner's office. I loved this man. I appreciated his willingness to bring me into his family business. Now I was about to drop the reality that I had done a wicked thing. He questioned me as to what exactly happened. The challenge for me was that the GM was in the room too!

I hemmed and hawed, and then he said, "We have zero tolerance for sexual harassment in this company. We should be high-fiving the greatest week in our company, but instead, I am going to ask for your business credit card and for you to immediately leave."

Wow! What had just happened? I tried to explain that the text was *not* intended for her, but in the end, the damage was done. I *had* sent the text, and motive was not important at this point. After only five months at this job, I was being escorted out like a criminal and asked to never come back.

I sat in my car, blown away. What was I to do? I had just lost my income to support my family. I had just blown my testimony, as the GM was not a believer. I had just fractured the trust of my friend who owned the company. And now I was going to have to go home and tell my wife what had happened.

I had stepped to the Edge, peeked over, and lost my footing. The fall was not so bad. It was the sudden stop at the bottom that really hurt!

Chapter 11

THE BOTTOM
Part 2

If you listen to these commands of the Lord your God that I am giving you today, and if you carefully obey them, the Lord will make you the head and not the tail, and you will always be on top and never at the bottom.

Deuteronomy 28:13 NLT

The drive home from the office seemed like a very bad dream. My mind kept racing as I thought, *how in the world did I accidentally send her that text?* The better question was: why in the world did I send that text at all? I came home to an empty house, as my wife was out of town (two hours away) at her sister's house for a few days. And now I was going to have to break the news to her. I wrestled with how much to tell her.

To avoid her freaking out, I simply explained that I had a big blowout at the office and was fired, and I would explain when she came home in two days. As it turned out, it was on her drive home that I ended up telling her about why exactly I had been fired. As I retold the story from that strange Wednesday night, a silence filled the phone with what seemed like 30 minutes of total silence.

"You sent a naked picture of yourself to another woman?" Heather said with pain in her voice.

"Of course I did not mean for it to go to her!" I emphasized.

But it did not matter at that moment. I had messed up **bad**! The reality was that I was about to turn 50, and now I had no job; it was weighing on my every moment of every day.

Today, I have four men with whom I share everything. In years past, I would share with them even if I felt the slightest pull to the Edge. I would talk about a feeling I had, or a struggle that was on my mind. But for some reason, I did not discuss what was happening with any of them until it was too late.

I first repented to God. A familiar Scripture is found in **1 John 1:9 NLT** that says, *"But if we confess our sins to him, he is faithful and just to forgive us our sins and to cleanse us* *from all wickedness."* Thank God for His forgiving power!

I chose to come to God much like David did in **Psalm 51:**

> 1 Have mercy on me, O God, because of your unfailing love. Because of your great compassion, blot out the stain of my sins.
> 2 Wash me clean from my guilt. Purify me from my sin.
> 3 For I recognize my rebellion; it haunts me day and night.
> 4 Against you, and you alone, have I sinned; I have done what is evil in your sight. You will be proved right in what you say, and your judgment against me is just.
> 5 For I was born a sinner — yes, from the moment my mother conceived me.
> 6 But you desire honesty from the womb, teaching me wisdom even there.
> 7 Purify me from my sins, and I will be clean; wash me, and I will be whiter than snow.
> 8 Oh, give me back my joy again; you have broken me—now let me rejoice.
> 9 Don't keep looking at my sins. Remove the stain of my guilt.
> 10 Create in me a clean heart, O God. Renew a loyal spirit within me.
> 11 Do not banish me from your presence, and don't take your Holy Spirit from me.
> 12 Restore to me the joy of your salvation, and make me willing to obey you.
> 13 Then I will teach your ways to rebels, and they will return to you.
>
> **PSALM 51:1–13 NLT**

I am still so moved by verses 12 and 13! It is the driving force for me to write this book. Some of you reading this are currently rebels. You need to get away from the Edge and repent! You need to humble yourself and ask God to forgive you. And you need to STOP doing what you are doing!

But we need to also link **1 John 1:9** with its sister verse found in **James 5:16** that states, *"Confess your sins <u>to each other</u> and pray for each other so that you may be healed. The earnest prayer of a righteous person has great power and produces wonderful results"* (emphasis mine).

Over the years, I have shared this idea with hundreds of men. I have spoken with so many who hold things inside. I think most men hold things inside, certainly more than women do. But as a part of my healing, I found another man I could trust, and who trusts me, and we will confess to each other the things in our lives. I believe we ALL need that. I promise it will heal your soul.

It was amazing to see God reach right down amongst my mess and once again start to form a "mess"age.

So, one by one, I spoke with these men, who love me dearly — some by phone, some in person. I felt like a bum. I felt disgusted with myself bigtime, like I had let them down. Now, let me say this loud and clear: You do not have to tell everyone everything. The *why* is still way more important than the *what*!

THE BOTTOM Part 2

Once my wife got home from her sister's, she was not yet ready to communicate with me. She was cold to say the least. Can you blame her? I had hurt her once again! In fact, she said she did not know what she was going to do. Apparently, all the pain from nearly a decade ago was staring her back in the face. I had hurt her so badly then that she would rather be dead. Now she needed to reprocess all that had happened. As men, we can simply put things in boxes. We can open or shut that particular box as needed. But for women, everything is one box. The good news was that, over the years, God had totally and completely restored our marriage and our ministry. But once again, we were at another crossroads.

I felt alone, scared, and totally lost! Perhaps my life *was* ruined forever, like the voice I had heard had said that Wednesday night in Vegas. I thought many times about how I had blown it. I realized I might lose my family this time. There were many times I wept until it hurt. It was during this time that I spoke with each of my four best friends on a regular basis. I was trying to comprehend what to do. I needed help with how to interact with Heather. Their unified suggestion was to give her space, pray like crazy, and work hard at getting a much-needed job.

For nearly three weeks, I walked on pins and needles around Heather. I wanted so badly to hug her and to hold her, but that was *not* going to happen anytime soon. But she is an amazing prayer warrior and an amazing woman of God!

Then, one day out of the blue, she passed me a three-page note that basically said, "I am mad about you because of…." She then listed out many things that were points of pain for her. It was her way to get stuff off her chest. As I read the list, some of the things she mentioned hurt me. I wanted to defend myself at times. But then realized that I had once again hurt her. The circumstances were different, but nonetheless very painful.

It was amazing to see God reach right down amongst my mess and once again start to form a "mess"age. Heather's transformation through this process was amazing, and her journey with her Facebook posts became a work of art. And as I said earlier, God speaks to her in dreams. One day she came to me in the morning saying she had a dream. Here is her Facebook post from that morning.

> *I had a dream last night, and I vividly remember one line from my dream. "Do not throw any rocks at me please. I am not even holding any rocks in my hand." This reminds me of **John 8:7**…I feel like God is asking us to be quick to forgive those around us. Your spouse will hurt you — your family will hurt you — your friends will hurt you…BUT if they have repented to God and to you, then be QUICK to forgive. Walking in FREEDOM is what Christ wants for all of us! I am praying for those of you who are struggling with true forgiveness today … you CAN forgive … allow God to help you. **John 8:7** When they kept on questioning him, he straightened up and said to them, "Let any one of you who is without sin be the first to throw a stone at her."*

God has once again forgiven me and my foolish and carnal actions. Amazingly enough, so has my wife!

THE BOTTOM Part 2

This was still going to be a process. I was still going to have to earn her trust back again. The next day she wrote this:

> Okay — this post is for the wives out there (and the wives to be).... God, please help us encourage, support, and love our husband. Help us not to focus on what our husband is or isn't getting right, but help us to focus on how we can "do good" to our husband and, more importantly, how we can ultimately please You. Help us to see our husband through YOUR eyes today! **Proverbs 31:11 (ESV)** "The heart of her husband trusts in her, and he will have no lack of gain."

Yep, I am one blessed man! We were actually laughing the other day when I said, "See, that is why God gave me you. I NEED you!"

To that, she said, "Well, why did God give me YOU?"

My response: "He must be mad at you...."

CHAPTER 12

THE BASIN
MY HEART REVEALED

Then He put water into a wash pan and began to wash the feet of His followers. He dried their feet with the cloth He had put around Himself.
JOHN 13:5 NLV

One of my Holy Spirit-filled, radical friends, Pat Schatzline, who wrote the Foreword for this book, spoke with me after I realized that I had, once again, fallen off the Edge. I felt compelled to connect with him and explain what happened, and he shared a few things with me that became huge parts of my healing. First, he said, "You have been in a season of an undisciplined life." Man, that was right to the point! So true. The things that I previously would do to avoid the Edge, I actually, for some reason, had stopped doing. Most of you reading this have no doubt heard the saying that the definition of insanity is doing the same thing over and over again, and expecting different results. Well, the opposite can be a positive thing. In other words, if we do the same things, we can expect things not to change.

I let my guard down, and I guess I thought I was just fine standing right on the Edge peeking over. The second thing Pat shared with me was an idea he had.

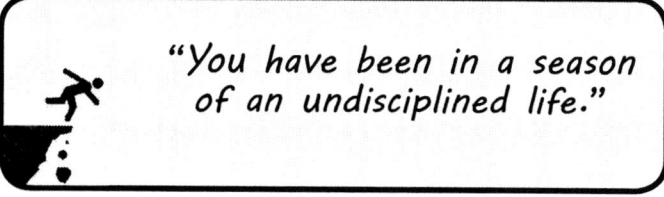
"You have been in a season of an undisciplined life."

"I think you should wash Heather's feet," he said with authoritative gusto. I had never thought of doing that! In fact, I had never done that, to anyone. I mean, I heard of Jesus doing that to show His disciples He was there to serve them. But me, never.

Pat said, "You need to wash your bride's feet, because you have made her walk through crap." Bam — this guy has my number. I immediately got a basin and a towel. That stayed on my sink for several weeks before I was released to use it. Or, should I say, before Heather was ready to receive the gesture.

You see, for weeks Heather and I had been working though the whys. What the heck was I thinking? She was allowing the Holy Spirit to work on her heart as He worked on mine. She needed to open up her heart once again to me, the guy who had hurt it now two times… badly!

It actually took a few weeks. As I mentioned a few chapters back, God speaks to Heather in dreams. Crazy, detailed dreams. She just plain knows stuff! God gave her such peace in her heart to trust me yet again. I was once again blown away by her mercy.

The night I decided was the night to wash her feet was a night we had scheduled to snuggle. In all fifteen years of our marriage, I do not believe that I ever asked her to put her robe ON. But this night was different. She walked into the bedroom with her robe on and quite the awkward smirk on her face. She is not one for surprises, and tonight was a surprise!

She sat in the chair in the middle of the room. I got on my knees and looked right into her eyes. Wow, as I write this, I still feel the presence of God in that moment! She had no idea what to expect, and to be honest, neither did I. I spoke directly from my heart to her heart, sharing mine as best I could. It was powerful for sure.

I repented again of the foolishness I had allowed to come into my life. I asked her to forgive me for the careless chances I took, and especially for not honoring her. Then we prayed together. It was one of the most amazing nights in our marriage. I was totally clean, and now her feet were too!

Maybe God is using this story to motivate you to create this amazing memory in your marriage. I have a friend about to celebrate his 44th anniversary who says this idea has sparked him on what he is going to do to celebrate their 44 years together. I guess he, too, had made his wife walk through crap! Maybe, as men, we all have.

Chapter 13

THE TRUTH
WHO GOES FIRST?

For if one of them falls, the other can help him up. But it is hard for the one who falls when there is no one to lift him up.
ECCLESIASTES 4:10 NLV

The climb back up the hill was easier in some ways this time than before, yet harder in others. I was very strong spiritually this time, so the walk back was much shorter. The part that hurt the most was losing my income. For 12 weeks, I had no job. And just turning 50 years old made it seem all the more difficult.

I have served as a very successful factory rep for several companies. I have owned my own businesses and then sold them for profits. I have worked in a leadership position for churches. I have been a vice president of a multi-million-dollar international company. And now I could not even get a job selling hammers at Lowe's. Yep, it appeared I was overqualified for most of the jobs I could find available.

My marriage was doing fantastic, but inside I was feeling so low; I knew that, once again, I had messed up, and this time, it was stinging really badly! The good news was we were in very good financial shape compared to most people. But the reality is it takes money to run a family with children and all that goes with their busy lives.

To make matters worse, I also had lost my insurance and that was hard to handle. But the good news is I had lots of time on my hands. So nearly every day I would meet with people, either for coffee or for lunch when people felt sorry for me. Some meetings were to see if they had any job ideas for me, but mostly it was to continue relationships with people. That is me. I love people.

I remember meeting with a prominent businessman in Orlando. I felt compelled to share my most recent situation. When I talked about me getting too close to the Edge, he got real quiet. Apparently, he, too, was close to an Edge. That is when he said, "Thanks for going first." That was an eye-opener. I was just talking and just trying to be honest, but that is all he needed to share some of his struggles of late.

Someone has to go first! Here is the deal: If I ever start creeping toward the Edge and I do not tell anyone, I will fall off ... every time! And the fact is, I will hurt many people around me in the process. I will hurt my family, my co-workers, my church, and even my own reputation.

Get this — a person can have thirty years of total perfection and then get too close to the Edge and slip downward. The sad reality is, that is all that tends to be remembered of them! Not the walk — only the fall.

Proverbs 27:17 NLT says, *"As iron sharpens iron, so a friend sharpens a friend."* But I know this: Iron fragments do not get sharpened when they are simply next to each other. No. They will only get sharpened by each other when they smash together! That is the part I missed too many times, when I never allowed another man to get close enough to see me and where I really was. Thus, I was not be able to make it.

I need someone to ask me how I am doing. And I mean really ask — and then know when I am lying. They should know where I am weak, and I should know the same about them.

Do you have such a friend? If not, you will fall off the Edge sooner than you would like to think!

I have heard in some Christian men's circles that you need an "accountability partner." I have got to be honest, that sounds strange, and most men will simply never let it happen! But accountability is a must to stay the course. Someone has to be first. Someone has to set the tone for the process for all of us to follow.

Here is a similar passage:

> **9** Two people are better off than one, for they can help each other succeed.
> **10** If one person falls, the other can reach out and help. But someone who falls alone is in real trouble.
> **11** Likewise, two people lying close together can keep each other warm. But how can one be warm alone?
> **12** A person standing alone can be attacked and defeated, but two can stand back-to-back and conquer. Three are even better, for a triple-braided cord is not easily broken.
>
> **ECCLESIASTICS 4:9–12 NLT**

If you watch the news or follow on Facebook, you no doubt have noticed that many men are getting too close to the edge and falling off. We've read of the stories of Josh Duggar, Ted Haggard, Tiger Woods, not to mention the scandalous behavior by our former president, Bill Clinton. Men seem to be self-destructing almost daily!

These tragedies add up to thousands of people being hurt. Hundreds of families are being crippled, and many destroyed. Why? Because men are getting too close to the Edge. They approach the Edge for different reasons: some just out of curiosity; others, sadly, out of rebellion; while for still others, some are careless and for some others, others there is a demonic pull toward destruction.

When Jesus was addressing His disciples He said of the devil,

> *The thief's purpose is to steal and kill and destroy.*

> *My purpose is to give them a rich and satisfying life.*
> **John 10:10 NLT**

> *Stay alert! Watch out for your great enemy, the devil. He prowls around like a roaring lion, looking for someone to devour.*
> **1 Peter 5:8 NLT**

So what is the answer? Why does it seem so difficult to *not* fall off the Edge?

I will never forget hearing about a man named Aron Ralston. He survived a canyoneering accident in southeastern Utah in 2003. He was climbing alone when he fell down a ravine. For days, he was stuck with no way to free himself. Thinking this was the end, he amputated his own right forearm with a dull pocketknife in order to extricate himself from a dislodged boulder. Aron was trapped for a total of five days and seven hours (a whopping 127 hours). After he freed himself, he had to make his way through the remainder of the canyon, then rappel down a 65-foot (20 m) sheer cliff face to reach safety.

It makes for a great story and a great movie, but it all could have been avoided! I realize the best way for this to never happen would be for him to never go on a mountain. But the fact is, we will all fall sometime and in some way. Hopefully, we will not have to amputate our own arm, but we *will* fall at something and at some time. *Everyone.*

I wish it were not so, but only Jesus made it out of that one. So how can we avoid the pain? Here is the very simple answer I have understood for me. I can never climb

> *I think a word like "accountability" has become strange and old fashioned. Too bad, because I think we all need it.*

alone! If Aron had a climbing partner, he would still have his arm! If David had someone else on the roof, Uriah would still be alive. If I ... and the list goes on!

Like Aron, I climbed my way out. But I did not do it alone. I am beyond thankful for God's grace and the love, support ... and forgiveness of my friends, family, and especially my amazing wife! It was not easy. In fact, there were many days I really just wanted to give up. I was losing thousands of dollars a month. Every month. I really had a difficult time seeing the answer. Oh, I was out of the canyon, so to speak, but I was still messed up from the fall.

I now work for an amazing company; I get to use my skills in sales to make a great living with my weekends off to share a message of hope with anyone who will listen. Big reality: Now is not forever!!!

I also realize that I have a responsibility to watch out for my brothers in Christ. Because if they fall off the edge, it not only hurts their families, but it also hurts the Church as a whole.

> *Don't look out only for your own interests, but take an interest in others, too.*
> **PHILIPPIANS 2:4 NLT**

THE TRUTH WHO GOES FIRST?

I think a word like "accountability" has become strange and old fashioned. Too bad, because I think we all need it. I pray you are accountable to someone. Someone who can ask you some hard questions. Someone you have regular connections with.

Years ago, I had a friend, Darren, and he and I used to ask each other these 10 questions on a regular basis. Because we knew the other would ask, this created an "I better not do this because I will give an answer soon if I do" kind of feeling.

1. Have you spent time in the Word and prayer?
2. Have you had any flirtatious or lustful attitudes or tempting thoughts, or have you exposed yourself to any explicit materials that would not glorify God?
3. Have you been above reproach in your financial dealings?
4. Have you spent quality relationship time with your family and friends?
5. Have you told any half-truths or outright lies, putting yourself in a better light to those around you?
6. Have you shared the gospel with someone this week?
7. Have you done your 100 percent best at your job?
8. Have you allowed any person or circumstances to rob you of your joy?
9. Have you taken care of your body though daily exercise and proper eating and sleeping habits?
10. **Have you lied to me on any of these answers?**

That may seem like a silly list, but it was powerful! You see, the reality is that someone needs to go first!

Like my pastor from Arkansas, Rick Bezet, used to always say, *"I would rather run the risk of embarrassing myself with a handful of people who love and care for me than to run the risk of embarrassing myself in front of a lot of people who could care less!"*

Chapter 14

THE START
Every Day

O God, You are my God; Early will I seek You; My soul thirsts for You; My flesh longs for You In a dry and thirsty land Where there is no water.
Psalm 63:1 NKJV

So how do you start your day? Whether you wake up to an alarm or simply by opening your eyes when you are done sleeping, what is the first thing you do? Well, for me now, I lay in bed and address each of the persons of the Trinity. Yep, I say good morning to the Father, Son, and Holy Spirit. Then I dedicate my life, my talents, and my day to God. I ask that He uses me, keeps me from danger, and allows me to show others His love.

I wish I could say I always do this. It actually seems that I am as I write this book. But for sure I have not always done this. I want to challenge you for a moment, maybe with more of a statement than a question. In my opinion, as witnessed by my own mistakes, I am convinced that being a disciple of God actually requires being disciplined.

> What are your desired results that you are expecting? If it is to honor Jesus and be His disciple, then the earth-shattering reality is this: You will need to be disciplined to accomplish that!

That is a scary word for most. It sure is for me! Now, my amazing wife, on the other hand, is the most disciplined person I know. It is just how she is wired. She was a college gymnast and then became a national fitness competitor. That takes lots of discipline!

I remember that while she was training, she would eat close to ten meals every day, and always at a certain time. Everything was intentional. Everything had a plan with a precise process to accomplish her desired end results.

So let me ask you a personal question: What are your desired results that you are expecting? If it is to honor Jesus and be His disciple, then the earth-shattering reality is this: You will need to be disciplined to accomplish that!

If you are a parent, you know what discipline is — or at least you should. When I was a child, I hated to be disciplined because I am a people-pleaser. When I needed to be disciplined, it was because I did not "please" a person.

Here is what Proverbs 12:1 NLT says: *"To learn, you must love discipline; it is stupid to hate correction."* Well, that sums it up, doesn't it? Isn't it interesting that the words disciple, discipline, and disciplined all have the same root word? So part of the deal to accomplish our desired outcome is to be disciplined. Here is how Paul parallels this idea with an athlete like my wife:

> 24 Don't you realize that in a race everyone runs, but only one person gets the prize? So run to win!
> 25 All athletes are disciplined in their training. They do it to win a prize that will fade away, but we do it for an eternal prize.
> 26 So I run with purpose in every step. I am not just shadowboxing.
> 27 I discipline my body like an athlete, training it to do what it should. Otherwise, I fear that after preaching to others I myself might be disqualified.
> **1 CORINTHIANS 9:24–27 NLT**

If you have been a follower of Jesus for any length of time, you know what the disciplines are to be a faithful Christian:

- Prayer
- Bible study and memorization
- Worship
- Fellowship with believers
- Evangelism
- Giving
- Serving

I don't think they need much explanation. If they do for you, there are plenty of books to help with these. Bottom line, we simply need to practice doing these spiritual disciplines or get ready for God's discipline!

CHAPTER 15

THE ASSIGNMENT
OLD MAN...DIE!

Those of us who belong to Christ have nailed our sinful old selves on His cross. Our sinful desires are now dead.
GALATIANS 5:24 NLV

I recently had a question for myself: "Do I hate sin?" At first I said, "Of course I do!" I mean, that is the correct answer, isn't it? Look at what Paul said to the Romans:

> 6 We know that our old sinful selves were crucified with Christ so that sin might lose its power in our lives. We are no longer slaves to sin.

7 For when we died with Christ we were set free from the power of sin.
8 And since we died with Christ, we know we will also live with him.
9 We are sure of this because Christ was raised from the dead, and he will never die again. Death no longer has any power over him.
10 When he died, he died once to break the power of sin. But now that he lives, he lives for the glory of God.
11 So you also should consider yourselves to be dead to the power of sin and alive to God through Christ Jesus.
12 Do not let sin control the way you live; do not give in to sinful desires.
13 Do not let any part of your body become an instrument of evil to serve sin. Instead, give yourselves completely to God, for you were dead, but now you have new life. So use your whole body as an instrument to do what is right for the glory of God.
14 Sin is no longer your master, for you no longer live under the requirements of the law. Instead, you live under the freedom of God's grace.
ROMANS 6:6–14 NLT

It appears that sin comes from the "old man." It also seems like my "flesh" was crucified with Jesus on the cross! Once and for all. If I sin now, after I have given my life to Jesus and let His blood cleanse all my filth, then I *willfully disobey God*.

20 But that isn't what you learned about Christ.
21 Since you have heard about Jesus and have learned the truth that comes from him,

> 22 throw off your old sinful nature and your former way of life, which is corrupted by lust and deception.
> 23 Instead, let the Spirit renew your thoughts and attitudes.
> 24 Put on your new nature, created to be like God — truly righteous and holy.
> **EPHESIANS 4:20-24 NLT**

Perhaps when I grasp the progression of sin, it will help me determine where I am in the process. There seem to be five levels, or stages, of sin. **Psalm 19** seems to reveal this hidden truth. I want you to see it in the Amplified Bible to really get a handle of the key words.

> 9 The [reverent] fear of the Lord is clean, enduring forever; the ordinances of the Lord are true and righteous altogether.
> 10 More to be desired are they then gold, even than much fine gold; they are sweeter also than honey and drippings from the honeycomb.
> 11 Moreover, by them Your servant is warned [reminded, illuminated, and instructed]; and in keeping them there is great reward.
> 12 Who can discern his lapses and <u>**errors**</u>? Clear me from <u>**hidden (unconscious, unintended) faults**</u>.
> 13 Also keep back Your servant from <u>**presumptuous (deliberate, willful) sins**</u>; let them not have control over me! Then shall I be blameless (complete), and I shall be innocent and clear of <u>**great transgression**</u>.
> 14 Let the words of my mouth and the meditation of my heart be acceptable in Your sight, O Lord, my [firm, impenetrable] Rock and my Redeemer.
> **PSALM 19:9-14 AMPLIFIED BIBLE (EMPHASIS MINE)**

This passage seems to indicate that there are five stages or levels of sin. I realize that all sin is sin in God's eyes, but I am referring to the way sin affects us as individuals.

In verse 12 it says, "*Who can discern his lapses and er-rors?*" I look at this as the ground floor, so to speak, of sin. An error is something that remains in our lives; it is wrong but is still present even after we have surrendered our lives to the lordship of Christ.

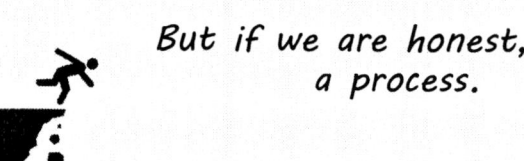

But if we are honest, life is a process.

After I gave my life to Christ, I was not made instantly perfect. I wish that were the case. I think many of my struggles occur because I have built up habits over the years, and now that my life is being changed with the power of the Holy Spirit, I still just do things out of habit. I know some folks who cuss to make a point. Or maybe some go drinking and then to a strip club with the guys to relax.

But if we are honest, life is a process. When I think about babies ... well, actually, I am not a fan of babies. I hope that is not too offensive, but they are so helpless. Not to mention, they poop in their pants! That is just wrong! We currently are caring for a two-year-old foster son. I love that boy dearly, but man, can he make a mess in his pants!

So what is my point? It takes time to get cleaned up. I realize that, for some, God does a number on you, and if you struggle with drugs, for example, he may just take the desire away forever. But it does not happen like that for everyone. One day, the Holy Spirit says, "Chris, that ____ (whatever it is), grieves me. Please stop doing that."

The second level is in verse 12 as well: *"Clear me from **hidden faults.**"* The Amplified version adds emphasis to the word hidden as "unconscious." This is when you are aware of the particular sin but you hide it. It is hidden in your unconscious mind now. You do not even think about it. However, this is when you start to sneak around. You know what you are doing is wrong, so you hide the secret the best you can.

If you keep on sinning and hide it so no one sees you, it will grow and turn into the next level in verse 13: "Keep back Your servant also from ***presumptuous sins***"

Presumptuous literally means *"to boil over."* I think of a stove with a pot on it and potatoes boiling. There's no problem until you put a lid on it. That is when it boils over. This is when the "our sins will be shouted from the rooftops" idea comes into play. Your secret will eventually boil over!

We see this all the time on Facebook and in the news. Someone is always watching and willing to tell the world, even if it is a fractured view of your situation. This is the time when most Christians deal with their junk. They have a choice to make: Either continue in their sin or repent and turn from it and be restored in the Lord.

If there is no repentance, then stage four follows. Verse 13 continues with *"let them not have **control** over me!"* That is exactly it. Now you are in trouble. Sin has taken you over — it now controls you! This is where the concept of a demonic stronghold comes from. The enemy has a stronghold on us.

This activity rules your life. It is all you think about. Your everything is all wrapped up in this activity. You know it, but now you simply cannot help yourself. You have stepped over the Edge.

Paul says in **Romans 6:14** that we do not have to let sin be our master. But when we continue to sin without repentance, we can fall into the highest level of sin, and that is the ***Great Transgression!*** This is when God says you are finished. We see this sad reality in **Romans 1**:

> *18 But God shows his anger from heaven against all sinful, wicked people who suppress the truth by their wickedness.*
> *19 They know the truth about God because he has made it obvious to them.*
> *20 Forever since the world was created, people have seen the earth and sky. Through everything God made, they can clearly see his invisible qualities — his eternal power and divine nature. So they have no excuse for not knowing God.*
> *21 Yes, they knew God, but they wouldn't worship him as God or even give him thanks. And they began to think up foolish ideas of what God was like. As a result, their minds became dark and confused.*

*22 Claiming to be wise, they instead became utter fools.
23 And instead of worshiping the glorious, ever-living God, they worshiped idols made to look like mere people and birds and animals and reptiles.
24 So God abandoned them to do whatever shameful things their hearts desired. As a result, they did vile and degrading things with each other's bodies.
25a They traded the truth about God for a lie.*

ROMANS 1:18–25A **NLT**

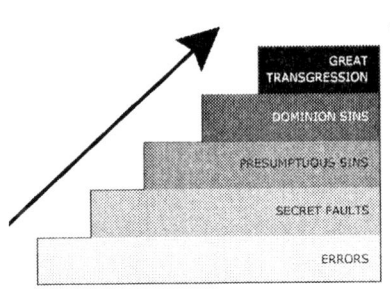

Like steps leading to death – we climb the steps of sin to the **EDGE!** If we journey to the top – it TOPPLES over and we die! Hurting the ones we love the most in the process!

CHAPTER 16

THE FACTS
MERE MEN?

But you are not like that, for you are a chosen people. You are royal priests, a holy nation, God's very own possession. As a result, you can show others the goodness of God, for he called you out of the darkness into his wonderful light.
1 PETER 2:9 NLT

I was in a group of people the other day and heard one of them say in reference to people struggling with a sin, "Well, we are only human you know." At first, it felt good to hear that; it would allow for me to live a less-than-what-God-has-intended path for my life. I could make all kinds of excuses for living for the desires of my flesh.

You can find what I will call "easy grace" in churches on nearly every block of our cities.

Please do not get me wrong. You have read about my life and know I believe in grace. In fact, I think that God decided to offer it because He knew about me! However, I believe it is time to turn up the heat on those of us who claim to be born again men. We cannot simply say, well, God's grace is sufficient for me, and live like we did when we were heathens (**Romans 6**)!

Apostle Paul was speaking to a group of Christians when he was writing these words:

> *1 Brothers and sisters, I could not address you as people who live by the Spirit but as people who are **still worldly—mere infants in Christ**.*
> *2 I gave you milk, not solid food, for you were not yet ready for it. Indeed, you are **still not ready**.*
> *3 You are still worldly. For since there is jealousy and quarreling among you, are you not worldly? Are you not **acting like mere humans**?*
> 1 Corinthians 3:1–3 NIV

The Apostle Paul seems to be a little frustrated with the Christians at Corinth. Paul says he wanted to address them as "people who live by the Spirit," but says he could not. They were "still worldly … mere infants." Ouch! Then in verse 3 Paul says, *"Are you not acting like mere humans?"* I realize that this particular section is addressed to people who are jealous and quarreling, but this really got my attention!

THE FACTS Mere Men?

After reading this out loud, I guess that our humanness cannot and should not be an excuse for us either. No more of me saying, "Well, I am only human, you know!" Check out what Paul says in **Colossians 3:**

> 5 So put to death the sinful, earthly things lurking within you. Have nothing to do with sexual immorality, impurity, lust, and evil desires. Don't be greedy, for a greedy person is an idolater, worshiping the things of this world.
> 6 Because of these sins, the anger of God is coming.
> 7 You <u>used to do these things when your life was still part of this world.</u>
> 8 But now is the time to get rid of anger, rage, malicious behavior, slander, and dirty language.
> 9 Don't lie to each other, for you have stripped off your old sinful nature and all its wicked deeds.
> 10 Put on your new nature, and be renewed as you learn to know your Creator and become like him.
> 11 In this new life, it doesn't matter if you are a Jew or a Gentile, circumcised or uncircumcised, barbaric, uncivilized, slave, or free. Christ is all that matters, and he lives in all of us.
> 12 Since God **chose you to be the holy people** he loves, you must clothe yourselves with tenderhearted mercy, kindness, humility, gentleness, and patience.
> 13 Make allowance for each other's faults, and forgive anyone who offends you. Remember, the Lord forgave you, so you must forgive others.
> 14 Above all, clothe yourselves with love, which binds us all together in perfect harmony.
> 15 And let the peace that comes from Christ rule in your hearts. For as members of one body you are

called to live in peace. And always be thankful.
16 Let the message about Christ, in all its richness, fill your lives. Teach and counsel each other with all the wisdom he gives. Sing psalms and hymns and spiritual songs to God with thankful hearts.
17 And whatever you do or say, do it as a representative of the Lord Jesus, giving thanks through him to God the Father.
COLOSSIANS 3:5-17 NLT (EMPHASIS MINE)

That pretty much says it all. I know it is easier said than done — just read the last few chapters of this book! But get this — if we could not accomplish this, why would God have asked us to do it? News flash: He wouldn't!

We all know we cannot accomplish this in our own strength. So how can we practically go through life and not struggle every day while desiring to please our flesh?

21 Since you have heard about Jesus and have learned the truth that comes from him,
*22 **throw off your old sinful nature** and your former way of life, which is corrupted by lust and deception.*
*23 Instead, let the Spirit **renew your thoughts and attitudes.***
24 Put on your new nature, created to be like God — truly righteous and holy.
EPHESIANS 4:21-24 NLT (EMPHASIS MINE)

Perhaps the biggest hang-up we as church people have is that we think Christianity is an event. But I have come to realize Christianity is a *lifestyle*. We should not get frustrated just because we said a prayer when we were eight

THE FACTS MERE MEN?

— because the preacher said if we didn't, we would burn in a hot hell where even the worms do not die, and there is no water, but only people screaming — forever!

Perhaps we missed it. It is not merely a "decision." It is a total surrender to God's will and not mine. And this is not about a one-time confession, but every day! *That* is lordship. He is in control. He is *my* Lord and savior.

So let's continue to get real. For me, it seems like I go through seasons. Sometimes it is easier for me to live a holy life unto God. But then there are other times — maybe it is just me — when I struggle like CRAZY.

> *And this is not about a one-time confession, but every day! That is lordship. He is in control. He is my Lord and savior.*

That is why we never give up. Though our bodies are dying, our spirits are being renewed every day.
2 CORINTHIANS 4:16 NLT

We are *not* "mere humans." No, we are blood-bought children of God standing on the rock, Christ Jesus! Paul shows us the comparison between being controlled by the flesh and being controlled by the Spirit in his book to the Galatians, chapter 5.

> 19 When you follow the desires of your sinful nature, the results are very clear: sexual immorality,

> impurity, lustful pleasures,
> 20 idolatry, sorcery, hostility, quarreling, jealousy, outbursts of anger, selfish ambition, dissension, division,
> 21 envy, drunkenness, wild parties, and other sins like these. Let me tell you again, as I have before, that anyone living that sort of life will not inherit the Kingdom of God.
> 22 But the Holy Spirit produces this kind of fruit in our lives: love, joy, peace, patience, kindness, goodness, faithfulness,
> 23 gentleness, and self-control. There is no law against these things!
> 24 Those who belong to Christ Jesus have nailed the passions and desires of their sinful nature to his cross and crucified them there.
> 25 Since we are living by the Spirit, let us **follow the Spirit's leading** in every part of our lives.
>
> **GALATIANS 5:19–26 NLT (EMPHASIS MINE)**

The Amplified Bible says of verse 25: "If we [claim to] live by the [Holy] Spirit, let us also walk by the Spirit. [If by the Holy Spirit we have our life in God, let us go forward walking in line, our conduct controlled by the Spirit.]"

GALATIANS 5:25 AMP

This literally means to march in a line like in the military. It is done with precision. It is done with purpose!

> For God called you to do good, even if it means suffering, just as Christ suffered for you. He is your example, and you must follow in his steps.
>
> **1 PETER 2:21 NLT**

CHAPTER 17

THE HOPE
Our Guardrails

Therefore, put on every piece of God's armor so you will be able to resist the enemy in the time of evil. Then after the battle you will still be standing firm.
EPHESIANS 6:13 NLT

So let's get practical. If we are honest, we all have an Edge (or more than one) in our lives that we need to avoid. These are weaknesses that either we were born with or we have allowed to grow in our lives and become an Edge of danger.

For you, it may be painkillers (even if they are prescribed by a doctor). Elvis had this Edge in his life, and in the end, he fell off and died. Maybe your Edge is alcohol. Or maybe you have the need to be accepted and you love when people like you. That need for acceptance could be an Edge just waiting for you to fall off of it!

Even if we are committed to staying away from the Edge, it is a great idea to set up guardrails. This will help to keep us safe should we become careless when going through life maybe a little too fast.

G – Goals: Know what you want to avoid.

U- Unique: Each person's "guardrails" are different.

A – Accountability: Have close friends that ask tough questions.

R – Real: Get real with yourself about your shortcomings.

D – Deep: Not just surface stuff.

R – Relationships: Goes both ways — be a friend to others to point out the Edges.

A – Action: Take action when things are pointed out to you.

I – Inspect: Look at your life regularly to prevent blind spots.

L – Love: Love others and yourself through the process.

THE HOPE Our Guardrails

> *You see, the ultimate way to not fall off the Edge is to stay far away from it forever!*

If there were a 1,200-foot cliff on a road and you wanted your family to pass by on it, wouldn't you want a guardrail? Of course you would! I heard a story a long time ago about three men who applied for a job driving a stagecoach over a mountain pass with a narrow road on the edge of a cliff.

The owner of the stagecoach line had each man drive the stage once over the pass; then he asked each man the same question: "How close to the edge did you drive?"

The first man answered, "I drove within one foot of the edge!"

The second man answered, "I drove within six inches of the edge!"

The third man answered, "I drove as far from the edge as I could get."

Guess who got hired? Yep ... the third man, because the owner wanted to ensure that the wagon would arrive safely at its destinations without falling off the edge. You see, the ultimate way to not fall off the Edge is to stay far away from it forever!

The time to make a decision about how far you will go with your girlfriend is *not* in the back seat after ten minutes of heavy kissing. No! It is before you even ask any girl out. We men are not so good at making quality decisions in the heat of the moment.

That is why we need guardrails. Make sure you have yours along your Edge, and double check that they are not broken since the last time you ran through it going too fast and being careless. Do it for God. Do it for the ones you love. Do it for yourself.

I remember my pastor sharing a story about a man who was struggling with looking at pornography. He would do good for a short season, then fall again. He asked Pastor Rick if he would come to his office and pray over it, as that is where he would struggle. When Rick got to the office, he noticed how the room was set up. That is when God showed him the practical answer. Rick said, "Do you want to be cured from looking at pornography forever?" The man eagerly agreed. That is when Rick turned his desk around so the computer screen would face the big glass window that pointed to the outside.

So simple — but it worked! That is a guardrail. For you, it may be that easy — or it may not be. But it is so totally worthwhile to have set guardrails before you go over the Edge.

For me? Every email and every text message is available for my wife to see in real time on the synced computer at home. The computers are all linked together, and that makes it impossible to get away with any Edge creeping.

CHAPTER 18

THE PROMISE
NOT CHEAP GRACE!

God saved you by his grace when you believed. And you can't take credit for this; it is a gift from God.
EPHESIANS 2:8 NLT

I thank God for His grace! I realize I could not have come to God without it. I am talking about needing His grace on an ongoing basis, but I do not take this gift lightly. God knew when He made Adam that He was taking a risk. If you think about it, it seems like God's first plan was to simply give Adam some animals to play and hang with. But it did not take Adam long before he became bored. That is when God made Adam his helpmate, Eve. Of course, Adam would never be bored again. After God made Eve, He presented her to Adam, and just as he was in charge of naming all the animals, Adam named Eve. He saw her — naked — and called, "WO'...Maaaan!" Ha!

To gain a better understanding of God's grace and what it means to us, I suggest we take a good look at **Romans 6**. Here Paul digs into the grace of God. Paul says it perfectly:

> *1 Well then, should we keep on sinning so that God can show us more and more of his wonderful grace? 2 Of course not! Since we have died to sin, how can we continue to live in it?*
>
> **ROMANS 6:1-2 NLT**

I have been guilty of taking God's amazing gift of grace for granted. Or maybe a better way to say it is that I took advantage of it. When I surrendered my life to Jesus and made Him my Lord, that meant I surrendered my will to His will. That means I made Him my *complete controller.*

Here is how Paul addresses this:

> *12 Do not let sin control the way you live; do not give in to sinful desires.*
> *13 Do not let any part of your body become an instrument of evil to serve sin. Instead,* <u>**give yourselves completely to God**</u>*, for you were dead, but now you have new life. So use your whole body as an instrument to do what is right for the glory of God.*
> *14 Sin is no longer your master, for you no longer live under the requirements of the law. Instead, you live under the freedom of God's grace.*
>
> **ROMANS 6:12-14 NLT (EMPHASIS MINE)**

THE PROMISE Not Cheap Grace!

Then, if I stop being disciplined, that is when I take a trip to the edge.

Here is the concern I currently have with many mainstream churches. From my perspective, they give God's grace away like it is candy. Now, it is true that grace is free for us, but it was *not* free for Jesus. In fact, it cost Him everything! So please, if you desire to serve the Lord, and if you desire to be a witness, then be very careful with God's grace because it is a costly gift.

It may be the most precious resource we will ever have available to us. Please do not preach cheap grace, easy grace, or forever grace. None of these are real. You see, if we sin and keep doing the same sin knowing that we sin regardless of the Holy Spirit's conviction, then John suggests we do not even know God for real.

> *4 Everyone who sins is breaking God's law, for all sin is contrary to the law of God.*
> *5 And you know that Jesus came to take away our sins, and there is no sin in him*
> *6 Anyone who continues to live in him will not sin.* **But anyone who keeps on sinning does not know him or understand who he is.**
>
> **1 JOHN 3:4-6 NLT (EMPHASIS MINE)**

The fact is that we all sin. Hopefully, as we all grow in the maturity of the Lord, we sin less and less. I know, for me, that I seem to have seasons of victory. Then, if I stop being disciplined, that is when I take a trip to the edge.

Maybe you are friends with a person who claims to be a follower of Christ, and they are actively still participating in sin. And you know it because you and this person have had a conversation about it. Then you need to follow Matthew's advice:

> *15 "If another believer sins against you, go privately and point out the offense. If the other person listens and confesses it, you have won that person back.*
> *16 But if you are unsuccessful, take one or two others with you and go back again, so that everything you say may be confirmed by two or three witnesses.*
> *17 If the person still refuses to listen, take your case to the church. Then if he or she won't accept the church's decision, treat that person as a pagan or a corrupt tax collector."*
>
> **Matthew 18:15–17 NLT**

Sounds pretty harsh, but if followed, it works. Perhaps the biggest challenge with church folks, even some in leadership, is that they can feel "empowered" by some juicy information they received about the sinning person. And rather than go to that person directly like the Word tells us to, they tell another person what they know or heard. This gossip is oftentimes disguised as a "prayer request."

> *16 There are six things the Lord hates, seven that are detestable to him:*
> *17 haughty eyes, a lying tongue, hands that shed innocent blood,*
> *18 a heart that devises wicked schemes, feet that are quick to rush into evil,*

19 a false witness who pours out lies and a person who stirs up conflict in the community.
Proverbs 6:16–19 NIV

So many church folks have been guilty of this, and many families have been destroyed because the Word was not followed with reverence.

16 So from now on we regard no one from a worldly point of view. Though we once regarded Christ in this way, we do so no longer.
17 Therefore, if anyone is in Christ, the new creation has come: The old has gone, the new is here!
18 All this is from God, who reconciled us to himself through Christ and gave us the ministry of reconciliation:
19 that God was reconciling the world to himself in Christ, not counting people's sins against them. And he has committed to us the message of reconciliation.
20 We are therefore Christ's ambassadors, as though God were making his appeal through us. We implore you on Christ's behalf: Be reconciled to God.
21 God made him who had no sin to be sin for us, so that in him we might become the righteousness of God.
2 Corinthians 5:16–21 NIV

Chapter 19

THE RESCUE
Helping Others Up

We are glad whenever we are weak but you are strong; and our prayer is that you may be fully restored.
2 Corinthians 13:9 NIV

At one time or another, we will all need to repent and follow the path that King David took in **Psalm 51**. Perhaps we will take some time to restart, refocus, and recommit. Maybe reset our priorities. And if we were involved with ministry, we may also need to have the leadership of our local church restore us back to function in ministry. Here is how Paul describes it:

*1 Dear brothers and sisters, if another believer is overcome by some sin, you who are godly should **gently and humbly** help that person back onto the right path. And be careful not to fall into the same temptation yourself.*
2 Share each other's burdens, and in this way obey the law of Christ.
3 If you think you are too important to help someone, you are only fooling yourself. You are not that important.

GALATIANS 6:1–3 NLT (EMPHASIS MINE)

> *We need to restore the fallen. The church is filled with messed up men just like me.*

Isn't this amazing? I am especially drawn to the part that says this process should be gentle, or you (the people involved with the process) could fall into the same thing! Then we are to bear each other's burdens. How do we do that? Find a friend to let them know that the Edge is a scary place. My advice? Stay as far away from the Edge as you can. Oh yeah, and help others to stay far away as well. And if you fall off, or if a friend does, there is always a way back up. It takes time. It takes effort. And I do not believe it can be accomplished alone. How much time? How much effort? Each of our stories and each of our Edges are different. Not to mention, each of us can fall from different heights based on our current sphere of influence.

I am not sure there is a perfect model for us to follow. I do know this, however: We need to restore the fallen. The church is filled with messed up men just like me. Thank God for His grace. And thank God for people that get it! I need a savior, not for a one-time experience, but for every day!

But also know this: There is a real devil. There are real demons. There are real generational curses that can cause us to be bent toward a certain behavior. And for some of us, our friends are not the best influence on us at times. But the bottom line is that we are ultimately responsible for our own actions! And to be even blunter, we are also responsible for where we currently are.

I remember hearing a story about an older couple riding in their car. As they were heading down the road, the wife said to her husband, "Remember when we were first together and how close we would sit when you drove?" He looked at her and said, "I do. But I have not moved..." That is how it is with our relationship with God. He is in the same place. Where are we?

> *Don't be misled — you cannot mock the justice of God. You will always harvest what you plant.*
> **GALATIANS 6:7 NLT**

Chapter 20

THE POSSIBILITY
True Freedom!

So if the Son sets you free, you are truly free.
John 8:36 NLT

Most books start out with the good stuff first and the stuff to fill at the end. I hope you don't see that here. Actually, this is the most potent part of the entire book!

"I just want to be FREE!" my friend said to me as we talked about his struggle with lust. I thought about this verse that, if Jesus, the Son of God, sets you free, well then, by golly, YOU ARE FREE! Or at least should be … right?

So what is the deal? If he is not free or, to be a little more personal, if I am not free, then we must have not been set free by Jesus. Or maybe the Bible is a lie ... Many men have written about being free. They quote a bunch of Bible verses, then, sadly, as time rolls on, it is later discovered that many of those authors were actually *not* free after all! Is anyone? Can anyone be? Look what Paul says,

> *So Christ has truly set us free. Now make sure that you stay free, and don't get tied up again in slavery to the law.*
>
> **GALATIANS 5:1 NLT**

Apparently, we can become free, but I have learned over the years that it is not a forever thing unless we make it so. I have been free — for minutes! No, really! I have gone 2.5 minutes totally sinless. So it *is* possible. But could we go for hours? For days? For months? What about for years?

What holds us back? I think the number one thing that holds us back is our own past failures. I remember hearing about a man by the name of Roger Bannister. On May 6, 1954, Bannister was running for the Amateur Athletic Association in Oxford against runners from the university in their annual match. He ran with two friends who paced him, and then sprinted the last 200 yards for a record time of 3:59.4. Later that month, Australian John Landy broke Bannister's record by less than a second. How could no one ever run a mile in less than four minutes, and then, suddenly, a few weeks later that record is beaten?

I believe it is our past failures that can keep us back from what we actually could accomplish. That same year, 1954, twenty-four other people ran the mile in less than four minutes. That just goes to show us that, when we recognize something is possible, it can shift our mindset about us being able to accomplish it as well.

I believe another thing that can hold us back from being totally free is our inability to allow the Holy Spirit to have full control over our minds.

> 2 And because you belong to him, the power of the life-giving Spirit has freed you from the power of sin that leads to death.
> 3 The law of Moses was unable to save us because of the weakness of our sinful nature. So God did what the law could not do. He sent his own Son in a body like the bodies we sinners have. And in that body God declared an end to sin's control over us by giving his Son as a sacrifice for our sins.
> 4 He did this so that the just requirement of the law would be fully satisfied for us, who no longer follow our sinful nature but instead follow the Spirit.
> 5 Those who are dominated by the sinful nature think about sinful things, **but those who are controlled by the Holy Spirit think about things that please the Spirit.**
> 6 So letting your sinful nature control your mind leads to death. **But letting the Spirit control your mind leads to life and peace.**
> 7 For the sinful nature is always hostile to God. It never did obey God's laws, and it never will.
> 8 That's why those who are still under the control of their sinful nature can never please God.

> *9 But you are not controlled by your sinful nature. You are controlled by the Spirit if you have the Spirit of God living in you. (And remember that those who do not have the Spirit of Christ living in them do not belong to him at all.)*
>
> **ROMANS 8:2-9 NLT** (EMPHASIS MINE)

Perhaps the most awkward reason — but way more common than we ever want to admit — for not being free is that we actually do not want to be free. Stings, doesn't it? But the problem with so many people I have spoken to is that they really like what they are doing. It feels good. Some even say that God will understand. However, the first step for me being free was for me to actually want to BE FREE. Then live free. Forever. I have heard author and counselor Bob Hamp say many times, "Freedom is living out who you were created to be."

Oh, it is not easy. But it *is* possible. Paul encouraged us to live just like Jesus, who showed us the way. And His Spirit prays for us and empowers us to do it. *If* we let Him.

But let's get this straight … Jesus did not come to Earth simply so we would stop behaving badly. No, Jesus came so we could BE FREE! He came so dead people could live — and then live life more than abundantly!

Perhaps you know the verse where Matthew quotes Jesus when He states, "Seek first to NOT sin…" WAIT! That is not what Jesus said in Matthew 6:33 NIV. No, what He said was:

THE POSSIBILITY TRUE FREEDOM!

Let's commit to pray for each other! I need it. And I just think maybe you do too ...

> But <u>seek first his kingdom and his righteousness</u>,
> and all these things will be given to you as well.
> (emphasis mine)

We seek His righteousness not simply by acting like Jesus, but rather by us being in Christ and being who we are. After all, we are human beings, not human *doings*.

My goal now? To avoid the Edge no matter what!

> 24 Don't you realize that in a race everyone runs, but only one person gets the prize? So run to win!
> 25 All athletes are disciplined in their training. They do it to win a prize that will fade away, but we do it for an eternal prize.
> 26 So I run with purpose in every step. I am not just shadowboxing.
> 27 I discipline my body like an athlete, training it to do what it should. Otherwise, I fear that after preaching to others I myself might be disqualified.
> **1 CORINTHIANS 9:24–27 NLT**

I have learned exactly what and where the Edges are in my life. I will do everything I can by the power of the Spirit of God and with the help of the guardrails I have set up, along with some key friends, to *never* go close to the Edge again! Let's commit to pray for each other! I need it. And I just think maybe you do too ….

So please take my advice and stay away from the Edge! But if for some reason you don't, there is always a way back up the hill!

Facebook - Chris Gingrasso
 Twitter - @cgingrasso
www.runFromTheEdge.com

GREAT BOOKS TO READ

Go and Sin No More, by Dr. Michael Brown. Regal Books 1999. The best book on not sinning—but it is a big, long book! Very detailed and lots of scriptures!

Every Man's Battle, by Stephen Arterburn and Fred Stoecker. Waterbrook Press 2005. Powerful and candid look at what we struggle with as men.

Pure Desire, by Ted Roberts. Regal Books 1999. Great book that opens candid pages of a past life of failure.

Temptations Men Face, by Tom L. Eisenman. Inter-Varsity Press 1990. Deals with the different things we as men struggle with and hits them head-on.

At the Altar of Sexual Idolatry, by Steve Gallagher. Pure Life Press 1986. Strong book that even gets into the reasons and core of the WHY.

Think Differently Live Differently, by Bob Hamp. Thinking Differently Press 2010. Bottom line, if we don't change the way we think, we will simply not change! Amazing book!

The Bondage Breaker, by Neil T. Anderson. Harvest House Publishing 2000. A true book on freedom. But beware — it can mess you up ... for good!

About the Author

Chris Gingrasso was raised in a small town in Wisconsin by loving blue-collar parents. Growing up as a Catholic — a Christmas and Easter attender — he did not have a deep spiritual understanding until one summer night when Chris met God face-to-face after the death of a close family friend. Chris' spiritual life continued to grow when he sensed the need to attend Bible college and become a minister.

Chris served as a youth pastor in two states, then went full-time on the road speaking at churches, camps, retreats and conventions all over the world. He was traveling nearly 200,000 miles a year, speaking 40 times a month, and his schedule was booked 2-3 years ahead with several weeks double- and even triple-booked. After nearly two decades of traveling, Chris has found his place in business in sales.

Chris and his wife, Heather, share their story of hope and forgiveness, when God allows, with families around the world.

You're Not Alone...

Now that you've read this book, hopefully you realize you're not the only guy on the planet who has struggled, failed and fallen short of your ideal identity and destiny."

For more encouragement, thoughts from Chris and information on where Chris is speaking next go to **www.RunFromTheEdge.com**

Sign up for our updates and latest insights. "

If you'd like me to speak to your men's group or next conference or corporate event, let me know. I do keynote events that are motivational, inspirational and practical! For more information go to **www.runfromtheedge.com/speaking**